||| MOVE IT!

WORKBOOK WITH MP3S

3

JOE MCKENNA

SERIES CONSULTANT: CARA NORRIS-RAMIREZ

Contents

Starter Unit

Grammar and Vocabulary • To be

1 **Complete the conversations with the correct form of *to be*.**

1 **A** *Is* Emma your sister?
 B No, she *isn't*.
2 **A** Where .... you from?
 B I .... from Sweden.
3 **A** How old .... your parents?
 B Dad .... 38 and Mom
 .... 34.

• Have

2 **Match the questions (1–4) to the answers (a–d). Then complete the answers with the correct form of *have*.**

1 Do you have any pets?   *d*
2 Do your parents have a car?
3 Does Bethany have red hair?
4 Do we have time for a sandwich?

a No, she doesn't. She ....
 brown hair.
b Yes, we do. We .... class
 in fifteen minutes.
c Yes, they do. They .... a big
 family car.
d No, I don't. I don't *have* any animals.

• *Be* and *have*

3 **Choose the correct options.**

1 Tamara *is* / *has* 16 years old.
2 My cousins *are* / *have* a big house.
3 Sorry, I *'m not* / *don't have* time to talk right now.
4 Sara's boyfriend *is* / *has* very tall.
5 Kevin *is* / *has* long brown hair.
6 My grandparents *are* / *have* very active.

• Possessive *'s*

4 **Look at the picture and complete the sentences with *'s* or *s'*.**

We're the Russell family. Our parents, Cathy and Matt, have three children. The [1] children*'s* names are Ben, Laura and Phil. (That's me, Laura, in the middle!) That's [2] Mom .... car, and you can also see [3] Dad .... bicycle. We have three dogs. The [4] dog .... names are Fido, Blackie and Moonie. That's our [5] family .... house behind them. We live at number 34, and our neighbors, the Watsons, live at number 36. Our dogs often run after the [6] Watson .... cat. Their [7] cat .... name is Smoky.

• *Is* and possessive *'s*

5 **Read the conversation. Look at the *'s*. Write *is* or *possessive*.**

A What**'s** your last name?   [1] *is*
B It**'s** Kennedy. [2] ....
A My aunt**'s** name**'s** Kennedy, too! Where**'s**
 the name from?   [3] ....
 [4] ....   [5] ....
B My father says it**'s** from Ireland.
 [6] ....

• Subject and object pronouns

6 **Complete the sentences with the correct pronouns.**

1 I'm going shopping. Do *you* want to come with *me*?
2 Stella's upstairs. .... 'll be down in a minute, and then you can talk to ....
3 Tom's working. .... 'll come home at two o'clock, and .... 'll have lunch together.
4 Are the children outside? Can you ask .... to come inside? .... need to take a bath.
5 We got a letter from Brian! .... always writes to .... in the summer.

• Possessive adjectives

7 **Complete the sentences with the correct possessive adjectives.**

1 We're from Japan. *Our* names are Yumi and Keiko.
2 He's the manager. .... car's parked at the front door.
3 I'm the new teacher. It's .... job to help you speak English.
4 That's Barry's bike. .... frame is made of aluminum.
5 She's a cyclist. .... name's Yadida.

• Common verbs

8 **Put the letters in the correct order to complete the text.**

Today we're reporting from our summer camp. There are a lot of activities here for teenagers. We can ¹ *climb* (mcibl) a wooden tower, ² .... (upmj) into the pool and then ³ .... (msiw) to the side. We can ⁴ .... (lyf) a kite, or we can ⁵ .... (lisa) in a small boat on the lake. Then, if we're not too tired, we can ⁶ .... (nur) around the lake or ⁷ .... (lypa) tennis with a friend. At the end of the day, there's always a good meal, where we can ⁸ .... (tea) as much as we like!

• Prepositions

9 **Look at the picture. Correct the prepositions in the sentences.**

1 There are two people walking ~~down~~ the hill.
                                    up

2 A man is fishing behind the bridge.

3 Two people are walking under the bridge.

4 There's a wall behind the parking lot.

5 There's a boy standing on top of the wall.

6 There's a man reading on the trees.

• Indefinite pronouns

10 **Complete the conversations with these words.**

~~anyone~~	anything	Everyone	everything
no one	someone	Something	

1 **A** Hello! Is *anyone* home?
   B There's no noise! Can you hear the TV
      or .... ?
   A No. It looks like there's .... in
      the house.
2 **A** The town is very quiet today!
   B Yes! .... is at home watching
      the football game.
   A Well, I need .... to take me
      to the station!
3 **A** Is .... OK?
   B No. .... is wrong with my leg.

• Everyday objects

11 **Match these words to the definitions (1–6).**

sweater	magazine	notebook
poster	wallet	~~watch~~

1 We use this to tell time. *watch*
2 This is like a really big photo. We often put
   it on the wall. ....
3 A book for writing in. ....
4 We keep our money in one of these.

   ....
5 We often read one in the dentist's
   waiting room. ....
6 This is a warm top. ....

• School subjects

12 **Match the school subjects (1–8) to the related
words (a–h).**

1 art   a kings, queens and wars
2 English   b guitars and drums
3 geography   c laboratory, experiments
4 history   d algebra, geometry
5 literature   e grammar, vocabulary
6 math   f Picasso and Van Gogh
7 music   g novels, plays and poems
8 science   h countries, mountains

• Present simple: affirmative and negative

13 **Make sentences in the Present simple.**

1 On weekends I / not get up / before ten o'clock
   On weekends, I don't get up before ten o'clock.
2 We / have lunch / at two o'clock
   ....
3 Tina / play / volleyball on Saturdays
   ....
4 Tony never / arrive / on time
   ....

• Present simple: questions and short answers

14 **Complete the questions with these words.
Then write the correct verb in the answers.**

Does	drive	~~have~~	like

1 Do we *have* any homework for tomorrow?
   Yes, we *do.*
2 .... Lucas work on the weekend?
   No, he ....
3 Do you .... living in the city?
   Yes, I ....
4 Do your parents .... to work?
   No, they ....

• Adverbs of frequency

15 **Rewrite the sentences. Put the adverbs of
frequency in the correct place.**

1 Sophie remembers phone numbers! (never)
   Sophie never remembers phone numbers!
2 Jo and Ian don't play tennis on Fridays. (usually)
   ....
3 I go to the movies. (hardly ever)
   ....
4 Susan orders chicken at the restaurant. (always)
   ....
5 We don't have time to watch TV. (often)
   ....
6 Ana and her friends go horseback riding.
   (sometimes)
   ....

• Numbers and dates

16 **Write the numbers and dates in words.**

1 60 seconds in a minute   *sixty*
2 Mar 1   ....
3 Jul 5   ....
4 365 days in a year   ....
5 1,440 minutes in a day   ....
6 100 years in a century   ....
7 Nov 22   ....

• Was/Were

17 **Choose the correct options.**

A [1] *Was /* Were you at school yesterday?
B Of course I [2] *was / were*!
A What about Mary and John? [3] *Was / Were* they at school, too?
B I'm not sure. John [4] *was / were* at school all day, but Mary [5] *wasn't / weren't* in math class.
A What time [6] *was / were* that?
B Math class is from 11:30 to 12:30.
A [7] *Was / Were* all the other students in math?
B Three of the other girls [8] *wasn't / weren't* there. They had a special volleyball practice yesterday morning.

• Opinion adjectives

18 **Complete the adjectives in these sentences.**

1 I hate this song. It's t*errible.*
2 That new horror movie is really s...................... !
3 This homework is so b...................... .
4 Yes, we scored! What an a...................... goal!
5 I'm sorry. That joke just isn't f...................... .
6 My mom loves r...................... books.
7 I think mountain biking is the most e...................... sport.
8 My little brother can be very a...................... .
9 This dress is too e...................... . I can't afford it.
10 This meal is really t...................... . Thanks!

Speaking and Listening

1 **Match the questions (1–5) to the answers (a–e). Then listen and check.**

2

1 Do you have a favorite school subject?   *d*
2 Do you live with your family?
3 Do you have any hobbies?
4 What kind of music do you like?
5 Were you at Tina's party last weekend?

a Yes, I was. We had a great time!
b Yes, I do. I live with my mother and my brother.
c I prefer dance music, and I also like soul.
d Yes. I really like art.
e Biking. I go out on my mountain bike every weekend.

2 **Complete the conversation with these phrases. Then listen and check.**

3

Boring	so her classes	To the library
Very funny	What's happening	What subjects

Liam What class do you have next?
Sally Science!
Liam [1] *Boring*!
Sally No, it isn't! I think science is really exciting.
Liam Not for me!
Sally [2]...................... do you like?
Liam Literature. And our geography teacher is fun, [3]......................are always interesting.
Sally True! Where are you going now?
Liam [4]...................... , to do some research on the Internet.
Sally Oh, really? You mean watch videos?
Liam [5]...................... ! You can't watch videos on the school computers.
Sally Anyway, are you going to Sonia's later?
Liam [6]...................... at Sonia's?
Sally It's her birthday party!
Liam A party? Awesome! What time?
Sally Seven thirty. But you need to talk to Sonia first!

3 **Read the conversation in Exercise 2 again. Choose the correct options.**

1 Sally *likes / doesn't like* science.
2 Liam likes *two / three* different subjects.
3 Students *can / can't* watch videos in the library.
4 Sonia's party is *today / tomorrow*.

Home Sweet Home

Vocabulary • Rooms and parts of the house

★ **1** Put these words in the correct column.

attic	balcony	driveway
landing	patio	yard

inside the house	outside the house
attic	

★ **2** Complete the sentences with the words from Exercise 1.

1 Our car's in the garage! You can park in the *driveway*.
2 If you want to play ball, go and play in the .... !
3 All my old toys and books are up in the ....
4 We have a big plant on the .... at the top of the stairs.
5 In summer, we often have lunch out on the ....
6 There's an awesome view of the river from the .... outside my bedroom.

★★ **3** Put the letters in the correct order to complete the text.

It's a wonderful old house. The date above the door says 1820. We had to put on a new ¹ *roof* (foro) last year after the winter storms. The ² .... (ginslice) are high, and some of them are made of wood. There's a ³ .... (freeclapi) in each of the bedrooms, but we don't actually use them. When you go into the house, you go through the ⁴ .... (lalhywa), and the ⁵ .... (ratsis) are on the left. My mom's ⁶ .... (efocif) is behind them. It's the room with a lot of photos on the ⁷ .... (lawl). Oh, and the ⁸ .... (agrega) has space for two cars. That's on the left side of the building.

★★ **4** Find the family treasure! Look at the picture. Complete the text with these words.

attic	fireplace	hallway	landing
office	roof	stairs	wall

Go through the 1 *hallway* to the ² .... at the end. Then go up to the ³ .... on the second floor. Go left and find the room with a high ceiling. This is the ⁴ .... Inside, you can see a desk with a computer, a chair and some books in a bookcase. There's also a ⁵ .... in the middle, and in the ⁶ .... next to that, there's a small door. It's not easy to see this door because it looks just like a painting. Open the door and go up into the ⁷ .... Be careful because there's only one small window up there. At one end, there are a lot of old boxes. Under the ⁸ .... , on a shelf above the boxes, there's a large envelope. Take it down, open it and read what's inside!

Vocabulary page 104

Reading

★ **1** **Read the texts quickly. Choose the best option.**

The texts are …

a a leisure guide to the city.

b advertisements from people selling their homes.

c answers to people who want advice.

★ **2** **Complete the sentences.**

1 themansells says her husband has a new *job*.

2 jenwatts has no problems with .... her car.

3 benstarkey has a .... behind the house.

4 stellabailey lives near a baseball ....

5 jenwatts often travels by ....

6 benstarkey goes shopping by ....

★★ **3** **Complete the sentences with the correct name.**

1 *stellabailey* can see a nearby park from her home.

2 .... usually takes the train to Manhattan.

3 .... and .... live near some good stores.

4 .... doesn't use public transportation very much.

5 .... doesn't have any problems with noise.

Internet forum

themansells:

We're a family of four and we're looking for a new home in the city. My husband's going to work in a new office, and I'm a hairstylist. We have two young children. Any suggestions for a good area?

jenwatts:

We live in an apartment in Brooklyn, about twenty minutes from Manhattan. There are buses every fifteen minutes, so we don't need to use the car every day. Parking isn't a problem because the building has an underground garage. The shopping's good in this area.

benstarkey:

Our family lives in a house in Queens, about half an hour by train from Manhattan. It's a quiet area, without much traffic. We have a small front yard, and a backyard with a patio. The children are sitting out there right now! I only use the car to go shopping, and I park it in the driveway, so it's all very convenient.

stellabailey:

We live in a rented apartment in the Bronx, near Yankee Stadium. At the moment, people are coming out of a baseball game, so it's a little noisy, but it's not so bad at night. The stores and restaurants are good, and we can walk to most places. Oh, and there's a nice view of a nearby park from our balcony, too!

Grammar • Present simple and continuous

★ **1** **Read the text and choose the correct options.**

He [1] *paints* / *is painting* houses inside and outside. Today he [2] *works* / *is working* in an apartment. First, he [3] *puts* / *is putting* all the furniture in the middle of the room. Then he [4] *covers* / *is covering* the furniture with a big cloth before he [5] *starts* / *is starting* work. At the moment, he [6] *paints* / *is painting* the edges around the ceiling.

★ **2** **Put the words in the correct order.**

1 Tom / Friday / goes / on / always / a / night / out
   Tom always goes out on a Friday night.

2 housework / He / doesn't / with / help / the / usually
   ....
   ....

3 weekend / you / What / do / on / do / normally / the / ?
   ....
   ....

4 music / to / Elena's / MP3 / player / her / listening / on
   ....
   ....

5 reading / bus / on / isn't / a / magazine / She / the
   ....
   ....

6 now / are / What / doing / you / ?
   ....
   ....

★★ **3** **Look at the pictures and write sentences.**

1 work / café / serve / coffee
   He works in a café, and now he's serving coffee.

2 live / small town / visit / city
   ....

3 sell / fish / talk / phone
   ....

4 repair / cars / take / break
   ....

5 drive / taxi / take passenger / station
   ....

★★ **4** **Complete the conversation with the Present simple or Present continuous form of the verbs.**

A Mike, is that you? Are you busy?

M Yes! (I/make) [1] *I'm making* dinner in the kitchen.

A You in the kitchen? But (you/not normally/cook) [2] ....
   .... ! Why (you/cook) [3] .... today?

M Because my (girlfriend/come over) [4] ....
   for dinner.

A So is it Italian food?

M No, it isn't. (We/only/have) [5] ....
   Italian food in restaurants. This is a special Indian meal.

A (you/mean) [6] .... Indian from India?

M Yes, of course!

A But isn't that very spicy food?

M Often, yes, but (it/not always/have to) [7] ....
   .... be hot!

A OK! Anyway, what's that funny noise I can hear?

M Oh no! The (meat/burn) [8] ....
   in the pot! That's what happens when I talk too much on the phone!

★★ (5) Make questions for the underlined answers.

1 The children are playing in <u>the attic</u>.
Where are the children playing?

2 Right now, we're <u>having a party in the garage</u>!
....
....

3 My sister's <u>studying abroad</u> this year.
....
....

4 Tom's talking to <u>a friend</u> right now.
....
....

5 I'm waiting for <u>a bus</u>.
....
....

6 My dad mows the lawn <u>every two weeks</u>.
....
....

7 We <u>clean the house</u> in the spring.
....
....

8 Yes, we do. <u>We have a fireplace</u> in the living room.
....
....

9 Kevin usually celebrates his birthday <u>in the basement</u>!
....
....

Vocabulary • Furniture and household objects

★ (1) Label the numbered objects in the picture.

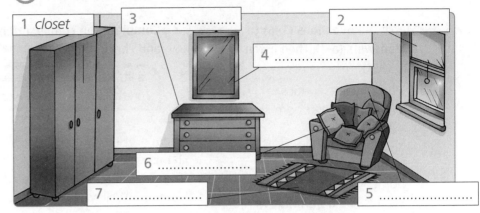

★ (2) Complete the sentences with the words from Exercise 1.

1 The *rug* is on the floor.
2 In front of the left wall, you can see a ....
3 In the corner of the room, there's an .... with .... on it.
4 Near the armchair, you can see a window with a ....
5 On the back wall, there's a .... with a .... above it.

★ (3) Match these words to the definitions (1–6).

| alarm clock | bookcase | ~~curtains~~ | comforter | pillow | vase |

1 We normally use two of these to cover a window.   *curtains*
2 We use this to wake up on time in the morning.   ....
3 We use this to keep warm in bed.   ....
4 We usually put flowers in one of these.   ....
5 We use this in bed for our head.   ....
6 We keep books and magazines in this.   ....

★★ (4) Put the letters in the correct order to complete the text.

This apartment's not bad! It has a big [1] *closet* (tesloc) for my clothes, and there's a [2] .... (koboseca) in the living room. I need that for my books because this month I'm taking a computer science course. And there's a desk but no [3] .... (cramhira), but I can bring one from home. What else? There's a [4] .... (rorimr) in the bathroom, but I don't see any [5] .... (stranuci) on the window, so maybe I can ask my mom to buy some. I don't like all those [6] .... (nisshuco) on the sofa—they can go in the closet in the bedroom. The bed's OK, but I'll bring my own [7] .... (remoctorf) and a couple of [8] .... (lowlips) because I'm more comfortable that way.

Grammar Reference pages 86–87

Vocabulary page 104

Chatroom Describing a place

Speaking and Listening

★ **1** Match the questions (1–6) to the answers (a–f). Then listen and check.
4

1 What's your school like?   *d*
2 What's your bedroom like?
3 What's that new shopping mall like?
4 What's your vacation home like?
5 What's Paula's hometown like?
6 What's that new café on Osmond Street like?

a It's very modern. It has three floors and a café on the roof.
b It's a little small, but they have really good music.
c It's pretty old, it's on the tenth floor, and it has great views.
d It's really big, with more than a thousand students.
e It's very big and really busy, with a lot of stores and traffic.
f It's pretty small, but very comfortable, and I have all my photos on the wall.

★ **2** Put the conversation in the correct order.

a And what's your room like?   ....
b So where are you living now?   *1.*
c Are you happy with it then?   ....
d It's very noisy and a little strange.   ....
e What's the city like?   ....
f Yes, but it's a long way from downtown!   ....
g In a rented room in the city.   ....
h Well, it's really cheap and pretty big.   ....

★★ **3** Complete the conversation with these phrases. Then listen and check.
5

| a little small | ~~Do you mean~~ | it like | kind of strange |
| pretty far | really wonderful | the house like | very big |

Olga	Hey, Tammi! How are you? I haven't seen you for a while!
Tammi	Hi, Olga! I'm just visiting and doing some shopping.
Olga	¹ *Do you mean* you don't live here anymore?
Tammi	Well, we have a new house on the coast, but I still come to visit my grandparents.
Olga	That's very good news! What's ² .... ?
Tammi	It's not ³ .... , just two floors, but it's in a really nice area.
Olga	I'm sure! And does it have ocean views?
Tammi	Yes. You can see ⁴ .... from the balcony upstairs. And it has a swimming pool too, but it's ⁵ ....
Olga	And what about the town? What's ⁶ .... ?
Tammi	Well, the house is ⁷ .... because it's five minutes from the beach. But the town is ⁸ .... , and my brothers and I miss our friends.

★ **4** Listen to the conversation in Exercise 3 again. Choose the correct options.
5

1 Olga and Tammi (know) / *don't know* each other.
2 Tammi *lives / doesn't live* with her grandparents.
3 Tammi likes the *location / size* of the house.
4 The balcony has *good / bad* views.
5 The house is *far from / near* the beach.
6 The children are *very happy / a little uncomfortable* in the new town.

★★ **5** Answer the questions about yourself.

1 What's your city or town like?   ....
2 What's your school like?   ....
3 What's your street like?   ....
4 What's your home like?   ....
5 What's your room like?   ....

Speaking and Listening page 113

Grammar • Verb + -ing

★ 1 Complete the text with the correct form of these verbs.

be	get	go	listen
rent	~~see~~	watch	

Living here is very easy. We enjoy [1] *seeing* the sunshine almost every day, and we love [2] .... able to sit outside for meals. We also like [3] .... for long walks in the countryside, which is close to our apartment. And we don't mind [4] .... wet when it rains, because it doesn't rain very often. As for going out at night, there are several movie theaters, although we sometimes prefer [5] .... a DVD at home. There's a theater too, although we don't go very often. I can't stand [6] .... musicals and I don't like [7] .... to classical music either!

★ 2 Put the words in the correct order.

1 apartment / I / stand / ground / living / in / an / on / the / can't / floor
I can't stand living in an apartment on the ground floor.

2 with / sleeping / on / She / the / light / prefers
....
....

3 watching / all / Grandma / TV / day / enjoys
....
....

4 housework / with / brother / hates / helping / the / My
....

★★ 3 Write sentences.

A Do you like living in Athens?
B I / enjoy / live / a big city
  [1] *I enjoy living in a big city.*
A And what about the weather?
B I / love / sit / outside in the sun!
  [2] ....
A And the traffic?
B I / not stand / drive / with so many cars / in the streets!
  [3] ....
A So how do you get around the city?
B I / like / ride / my bicycle!
  [4] ....
A What about the food?
B I / not mind / try / new foods!
  [5] ....
A And the language?
B I / prefer / speak / English!
  [6] ....
  Greek is very difficult for me!

★★ 4 Write sentences. Use the information in the table.

	😊😊 loves	😊 likes/enjoys	😐 doesn't mind	😠😠 hates/ can't stand
Justin	1 play video games	2 take the dog for a walk	3 wash the car	4 do housework
Leonor	5 get up late on the weekend	6 text on her cell phone	7 help her sister with her homework	8 clean the bathrooom

1 *Justin loves playing video games.*
2 ....
3 ....
4 ....
5 ....
6 ....
7 ....
8 ....

Grammar Reference pages 86– 87

Reading

1 Read the texts quickly. Match the text types (1–3) to the texts (A–C).

1 a postcard
2 a tourist advertisement
3 an offer of accommodation

A

Fuengirola
in the heart of the
Costa del Sol

Welcome to Fuengirola in the heart of the Costa del Sol, an ideal vacation destination! In winter, it's a quiet town of 72,000 inhabitants, with very fresh seafood and interesting places to visit. It's ideal for older people. In summer, it's a fantastic place for sun, sand and sea, with a population of 250,000 people! It's very popular with families and young people because there is so much to see and do. With shopping, restaurants, clubs, parks and a zoo—it has nearly everything!

B

VACATION APARTMENT FOR RENT in Fuengirola, southern Spain. Large apartment available for July and August. Three bedrooms, two bathrooms, kitchen and living room. Complete with balcony, underground garage and elevator. Fully furnished with beds, a sofa, armchairs and a TV. The kitchen's a little small, but most visitors eat out. For more information, please email fun_fuengirola@costadelsol.com.

C

Dear Mom and Dad,

Here we are, finally at the beach! The house we're sharing with friends is small, but we only come back here to shower and change before going out again. Maggie says she hates sitting on the beach all day, so she's doing a lot of sports. Tom loves doing nothing, so he enjoys lying on the beach and then going out at night. And I prefer doing a little of everything, so I read, listen to music, go swimming, go shopping ... and just relax! The weather's a little hot for me, so I don't go to the beach in the afternoon, but I'm having a wonderful time!

Love,
Linda

Brain Trainer

Underline these words in the texts in Exercise 1:
ideal
for rent
going out

Now do Exercise 2.

2 Complete the sentences.

1 Fuengirola has a lot of *older* visitors in winter.
2 In summer, 250,000 people .... in Fuengirola.
3 .... people can sleep in the apartment.
4 The apartment has an .... garage.
5 Linda and her friends don't .... much time in the house.
6 Linda .... go to the beach in the afternoon.

Listening

1 Listen to the conversation and decide who is talking.

6

1 a brother and sister
2 two friends
3 two office workers

2 Listen again. Choose the correct options.

6

1 The boy prefers the room *with /* (*without*) the balcony.
2 The girl *likes / doesn't like* the room with the closet.
3 The second room has a *bookcase / desk*.
4 The girl would like to have the *dresser / mirror*.
5 The boy wants a *dresser / desk*.

Writing • A description of a room

1 **Rewrite the sentences. Use the linking words.**

1 I like playing in the attic. I like playing in the basement. (and)
I like playing in the attic and the basement.

2 We enjoy sitting on the balcony. We like sitting on the patio. (also)

....

....

3 The cat loves hiding behind the armchairs. He's afraid of going down to the basement. (but)

....

....

4 That's his favorite pillow. He doesn't like using a comforter. (however)

....

....

5 We like having pillow fights. We like playing with cushions. (too)

....

....

6 I love lying on the floor to read. Sheena loves looking at the photos on the walls. (and)

....

....

2 **Look at the picture. Read the text. Correct four mistakes in the text.**

My dream room looks like this. It's pretty big and bright, and I can organize it the way I want.

The best things in the room are the bed with its comforter and the rug next to it. Opposite the bed is a bookcase with a TV on one of the shelves. On the wall above the bed there are posters of my favorite musicians and artists. There's a desk in the corner under a window. When I need to study, I just close the blind. On the wall, to the left of the window, there's a board for photos and notes. My papers and school stuff go in the drawers on the right of the desk.

I can lie on the bed listening to music. However, I also need time at my desk. When friends visit, we can play games on the TV, too.

3 **Read the room description again. Put these details in the correct section in column A.**

bright	lie on the bed
papers in the drawers	play video games
~~posters on the wall~~	pretty big

	A Picture room	**B My dream room**
Introduction		*My dream room has …*
Furniture and walls	*posters on the wall*	*There is/are …*
Activities		*I can …*

4 **Think of your dream room. Write phrases about it in column B.**

5 **Write a description of your dream room. Use your ideas and information from Exercises 3 and 4.**

What's the Story?

Vocabulary • Adjectives to describe pictures

★ **1** Put these words in the correct column.

beautiful	blurry	boring	colorful	dark	dramatic
fake	funny	horrible	interesting	old-fashioned	silly

one syllable	two syllables	three syllables
dark	*blurry*	*beautiful*

★ **2** Match the words (1–5) to the definitions (a–e).

1 blurry   *e*
2 boring
3 fake
4 dramatic
5 old-fashioned

a From another period in time, when life was very different
b It's uninteresting.
c It's not real.
d It's exciting; it makes me want to look at it.
e It's not clear; I can't see it very well.

★★ **3** Complete the conversation with these words.

blurry	boring	dramatic	fake	old-fashioned	silly

A Look at this! Look at those clothes! And the hairstyles!
B Where did you find that?
A In a box in the attic. The pictures are really ¹ *old-fashioned*.
B Yeah. I think they must be from the war or something.
A They're pretty ²........................ ! There aren't any colors.
B Yes, but sometimes they're very ³........................ . Here's one of a building on fire.
A And what's this one?
B I don't know! It's ⁴........................ , so I can't see the detail. It looks like a photo of a person's foot.
A Well, that's a ⁵..................... photo! Why would anyone do that?!
B Who knows! What about this one? It says "Love from Mount Everest, 1945."
A That's a ⁶........................ photo! Nobody climbed Mount Everest until 1953!

★★ **4** Put the letters in the correct order to complete the text.

There are many computer programs for working with photos. Users can create many kinds of ¹ *interesting* (gritsentien) pictures and effects with the software. You can completely change a ²........................ (floroluc) image by replacing the normal colors with a kind of brown, so you make the image look ³........................ (lod-fadishneo). Or you can change the clothes a person is wearing, and make the picture ⁴........................ (nunfy). Or again, you can make parts of the image ⁵........................ (ylrurb), so that one part becomes more ⁶........................ (cardamit). As people say, the only limit is your imagination! The only problem, however, is that it becomes difficult to tell the difference between an original and a ⁷........................ (kefa) photo!

Vocabulary page 105

Reading

★ (1) Match the photos (A–C) to the paragraphs (1–3).

★ (2) Complete the sentences.

1 Ulrike *changed* her clothes.
2 In the photo, Danny was ....
3 A storm .... into the beach last weekend.
4 Danny had his party in a ....
5 A tree .... on some cars.
6 Ulrike wasn't .... to the other people in the group.

★★ (3) Are the statements true (T) or false (F)?

1 There were a lot of people at Danny's party.   *T*
2 Danny's neighbors weren't happy about the music.   ....
3 Ulrike's group went to the beach last weekend.   ....
4 Nothing in Ulrike's backpack was dry.   ....
5 People at the beach were prepared for the storm.   ....
6 No one was hurt in the accident.   ....

Brain Trainer

Underline all the adjectives in comments 1, 2 and 3.

What do you notice about
a) their form?
b) their position?

Photos	Comments

A   **1**

Hi, guys! Here's a nice (but blurry) picture of Danny's birthday party! He was dancing really fast! There were about forty of us there. We used his parents' garage for the party. We stayed late, but nobody complained about the music. It was great!

B   **2**

Hey, everyone! Here are some colorful pictures from our hiking trip last weekend. My favorite one is of Ulrike falling into the water. She was crossing the stream and listening to music on her MP3 player. She didn't hear us warn her about the moving stones, so she fell in. She didn't hurt herself, but her backpack got wet, and everything inside it did, too. She changed into some dry clothes that Maria gave her.

C   **3**

How about this for a dramatic picture? We were at the beach last weekend when a sudden storm came in. The winds were really strong, so we left the beach fast. Then a big palm tree fell on some cars parked in the street. Luckily, there was no one in the cars. Adrian took this picture just five minutes after it happened.

Grammar • Past simple

★① **Match the questions (1–4) to the answers (a–d).**

1 Who took these photos?   *b*
2 Where did she take them?
3 What happened in this one?
4 Did they come out all right?

a Most of them did, but some are a little blurry.
b Jane did.
c It was at Fran's house, on Saturday.
d The flash didn't work!

★★② **Complete the text with the correct form of the verbs.**

This is a photo of my grandmother, who had an interesting life. When she was fourteen, the war started, and the family [1] *lost* (lose) their business in the city. Her parents [2] .... (not want) to stay in Wales, so they [3] .... (sail) to Argentina. They [4] .... (not speak) Spanish, but there was a Welsh community in Argentina, and her father [5] .... (find) a job there. My grandmother [6] .... (study) in Buenos Aires, where she [7] .... (meet) my grandfather. They got married three years later and had three children, including my father.

★★③ **Make sentences about Tanya's week. Use the information in the table.**

Things to do	Done ✓	Not done ✗
1 clean my room	✓	
2 wash Dad's car		✗
3 make birthday cake		✗
4 buy new shirt	✓	
5 reply to emails	✓	
6 check exam grades		✗
7 clean the fireplace	✓	

1 *She cleaned her room.*
2 ....
3 ....
4 ....
5 ....
6 ....
7 ....

• Past continuous

★④ **Put the words in the correct order to make answers.**

1 **A** Where were you last weekend?
  B on / I / the / volleyball / playing / was / beach
  I was playing volleyball on the beach.
2 **A** What about Saturday night?
  B club / I / friends / dancing / some / at / was / the / with
  ....
3 **A** Very interesting! And on Sunday morning?
  B newspapers / We / the /were / morning / reading / all
  ....
4 **A** And on Sunday afternoon, were you walking in the park?
  B We / park / walking / in / the / on / weren't / Sunday
  ....
5 **A** So what were you doing on Sunday?
  B We / an / old-fashioned / watching / were / on / movie / TV
  ....
6 **A** What were the people in the movie doing?
  B acting / silly / were / They
  ....

★★⑤ **Make sentences with the Past continuous form of the verbs.**

1 Some children / play / in the yard
  Some children were playing in the yard.
2 A dog / run / in the park
  ....
3 A man / park / his car
  ....
4 A young couple / do / their shopping
  ....
5 Some friends / take / photos
  ....
6 A neighbor / wash / his car
  ....
7 A cat / drink / milk
  ....

Grammar Reference pages 88–89

Vocabulary • Adjective + preposition

★ 1 **Match the sentence beginnings (1–6) to the endings (a–f).**

1 Stella's really good   *e*
2 Brian's very interested
3 Old-fashioned pictures are popular
4 Ella's excited
5 We're very proud
6 Jane's bored

a with some collectors.
b with the music on her MP3 player.
c in animal photography.
d of our school's prize in the photo competition.
e at taking dramatic photos.
f about seeing her photos in the school magazine.

★ 2 **Choose the correct options.**

1 We don't want to go to the mall because we're *proud of / tired of* going there!
2 Don't turn the light off! I'm *afraid of / bad at* the dark.
3 Our team won the game and we were *excited about / angry with* it.
4 She's a very nice person and she's *popular with / proud of* the other students.
5 Our teacher is really *good at / sorry for* telling stories.
6 I want to study music because I am really *bad at / interested in* it.

★★ 3 **Complete the sentences with these words.**

| ~~afraid~~ | angry | excited | interested | bad | sorry |

1 Everyone said they were *afraid* of traffic accidents.
2 He was .... with them because he didn't get a prize.
3 I'm usually .... at science, but I did very well on my last exam.
4 Everyone is .... about the next Olympic Games.
5 She was .... in becoming a writer.
6 Everyone felt .... for the parents with the sick children.

★★ 4 **Complete the text with the correct prepositions.**

This is an interesting picture! You can see this boy on the left: he looks tired [1] *of* playing with his toys. And the girl on the right, who looks bored [2] .... her doll's house. The other children in the middle are laughing and pointing at the screen. It looks like they're very excited [3] .... a video game. And look at the grandmother's face. She's very proud [4] .... her grandchildren! Finally, I feel sorry [5] .... the dog next to the boy. It looks afraid [6] .... the image of itself in the mirror! This is a nice picture because it is full of interesting details.

Vocabulary page 105

Chatroom Permission

Speaking and Listening

★ 1 Put the words in order to make questions. Then listen and check.

7

1 Lena / us / you / comes / mind / if / Do / with / ?
Do you mind if Lena comes with us?

2 bicycle / borrow / Can / your / I / ?

....
....

3 if / it / dog / we / OK / take / Is / the / ?

....
....

★ 2 Complete the conversation with the questions from Exercise 1. Then listen and check.

8

A Uncle John! ª ....
....

B What do you want it for?

A Kurt and I want to go for a ride.

B Yes, you can. Just be careful with the traffic.

A ᵇ.......................................
....

B Yes, of course! He needs the exercise.

A ᶜ*Do you mind if Lena comes with us?*

B Yes, I do! She has an exam in the morning, and she has to study!

★★ 3 Complete the conversation with these words. Then listen and check.

9

Do you mind if	I'm sorry	Is it OK	of course
~~popular with~~	you can		

Guide	Good morning and welcome to the Milefoot Country Park! This park is very ¹*popular with* people who love the countryside. We hope you enjoy your visit.
Man	Can we take photos in the park?
Guide	Yes, ²....................... . But we recommend that you don't go too near the animals.
Woman	Is it OK if we have a picnic somewhere?
Guide	Yes, ³....................... . There are special areas with benches where visitors can eat and drink.
Boy	⁴....................... if we go fishing in the river?
Guide	No, I'm sorry, it isn't. The fish are protected, and you can't catch them.
Boy	What about a barbecue? ⁵....................... we have a barbecue?
Guide	We don't mind if you have picnics, but ⁶......................., you can't have barbecues. It's too dangerous to light fires in the park.

★★ 4 Listen to the conversation in Exercise 3 again. Choose the correct options.

9

1 You can / can't see animals in the park.
2 Visitors *should* / *shouldn't* go near the animals.
3 Visitors can have picnics *anywhere in the park* / *in special areas*.
4 Fishing *is* / *isn't* possible.
5 Fires *are* / *aren't* allowed in the park.

★★ 5 Write a conversation. Use phrases from Exercises 1–3 above and this information:

You are staying for the weekend at a friend's house.
Ask permission to do three different things. Remember to include your friend's replies.

Speaking and Listening page 114

Grammar • Past simple vs Past continuous

★ 1 Match the sentence beginnings (1–5) to the endings (a–e).

1 I was having a wonderful dream   *d*
2 A ball hit a woman
3 The girl was texting on her phone
4 The boys saw a bank robbery
5 We were watching a news report on TV

a while they were sitting on the balcony.
b while she was walking through the park.
c when we recognized our friends at a concert.
d when the alarm clock woke me up.
e when she put her foot in a hole.

★ 2 Choose the correct options.

1 The weather *changed* / *was changing* while we came / *were coming* down the mountain.
2 We *ran* / *were running* through the woods when Angelica *fell* / *was falling*.
3 A bird *landed* / *was landing* on my shoulder while I *ate* / *was eating* a sandwich!
4 Marla *watched* / *was watching* TV when her friend *arrived* / *was arriving*.
5 I *got* / *was getting* a call while I *waited* / *was waiting* for the bus.
6 The passengers *sang* / *were singing* when the plane *took off* / *was taking off*.

★★ 3 Make questions for the underlined answers.

1 I was <u>listening to the radio</u> when I heard the news.
What were you doing when you heard the news?
2 I was listening to the radio when <u>I heard the news</u>.
What happened while you were listening to the radio?
3 Thieves were stealing a painting when <u>the police arrived</u>.
....
4 Thieves were <u>stealing a painting</u> when the police arrived.
....
5 My parents were <u>driving home</u> when the storm started.
....
6 My parents were driving home when <u>the storm started</u>.
....
7 Tania was <u>living abroad</u> when her parents moved.
....
8 Tania was living abroad when <u>her parents moved</u>.
....
9 I was <u>recording the concert</u> when the battery died.
....
10 I was recording the concert when <u>the battery died</u>.
....

★★ 4 Make questions for the missing information.

1 I was .... when I heard the news.
What were you doing when you heard the news?
2 Our team was .... when the rain started.
....
3 We were .... when the battery died.
....
4 Ana was .... when the phone rang.
....
5 My parents were .... when the mail carrier arrived.
....
6 The students were .... when the teacher entered the room.
....

Brain Trainer

Put *when* or *while* into these sentences:

I was drinking my coffee .... the email arrived.
The email arrived .... I was drinking my coffee.
Can you use either word in both sentences?
Look at Grammar Reference page 88 and write the rule.

Grammar Reference pages 88–89

Reading

1 Read the text quickly. Choose the best title.

a A Fun Trip to the UK
b A Dramatic Trip to the UK
c A Boring Trip to the UK

In the spring of 2010, my family was preparing for a trip to the UK. We wanted to go to Scotland to visit Edinburgh, and then to stay in London, to see all the famous places there. We were planning to stay for ten days, and I was really looking forward to the trip.
On April 10, we flew to Edinburgh and took a taxi to the hotel. The weather was colder than at home, but it was clear and bright. The next three days we went sightseeing. The dungeons on the Royal Mile were really cool! The 14th was our last day there, so we went shopping on the famous Princes Street. I got a photo of myself with a bagpiper in his kilt, and I emailed it to my friends. In the evening, we were having dinner when we saw pictures on TV of a volcano erupting in Iceland. The pictures were pretty dramatic, but we didn't worry.
The next day, we arrived at the airport for the flight to London. But we didn't catch the plane because all the flights were canceled. Why? Because the ash from the volcano was a serious problem for planes flying over the UK! In the end, we had to take a train to London, and we spent a whole week sightseeing and shopping in all the famous places. But we had to wait another two days before we could finally catch a flight home. Of course, that was OK with me, since I had an extra two days of vacation!

2 Read the text again. Put these events in the correct order.

a go back to Edinburgh
   airport   ....
b visit London   ....
c arrive in Edinburgh   1.
d see a volcanic eruption
   on TV   ....
e visit the dungeons   ....
f go shopping on
   Princes Street   ....

Listening

1 Listen to an interview with a girl who wants to be a photographer. How many photos do they talk about?

10

a 2   b 3   c 4

2 Listen again and choose the correct options.

10

1 The photo was of her
  brother's .... birthday.
  a second
  b third
  c fourth

2 The bird caught a .... .
  a mouse
  b rabbit
  c cat

3 She took the photo in
  Vermont in the .... .
  a spring
  b fall
  c winter

4 The colors in the photo
  were .... .
  a on the buildings
  b on an umbrella
  c in the streets

5 The two women in the photo
  were .... .
  a friends
  b sisters
  c mother and daughter

Writing • A description of a picture

1 Read the text and correct the sentences.

My mom took this photo about two years ago, when we were visiting my uncle. He lives in Spain, so we don't often see each other. He was living in a new house, and it was the first time that we saw it.

The photo is of a special meal. We cooked paella, which his family had never tried before. The weather was great, so we ate outside. You can see grass and some trees in the background. That's the food on the table in the foreground. That's my uncle and my cousin on the right, and my aunt on the left serving the food. My sister and I are in the middle. We're all laughing because my uncle was telling a joke.

I like this photo because it brings back good memories of the time we spent together.

1 This was the family's third visit to the uncle's house.
   This was the family's first visit to the uncle's house.

2 They ate in the kitchen.
   ....

3 The food is on the table in the background.
   ....

4 The people in the photo are crying.
   ....

5 Her uncle is on the left of the photo.
   ....

2 Read the text again. Put these phrases in the correct place in column A.

a special meal	good memories
in the background	in the foreground
in the middle	meal outside
new house	on the left
on the right	time together
~~two years ago~~	visit my uncle

	A Picture description	B My photo
Introduction	*two years ago*	
Who's/What's in the photo and where		
Reasons for choosing the photo		

3 Choose your favorite photo. Write phrases about it in column B.

4 Write a description of your photo. Use your ideas and information from Exercises 2 and 3.

(Introduction)

....
....
....

(Description)

....
....
....
....
....
....

(Conclusion)

....
....
....

(3) It's a Bargain!

Vocabulary • Shopping nouns

★ (1) Match (1–6) to (a–f) to make nouns.

1 dollar	a vendor
2 down	b basket
3 fruit	c bill
4 market	d stand
5 sales	e town
6 shopping	f person

★ (2) Complete the sentences with the nouns from Exercise 1.

1 We often go to the market. One of our friends is a *market vendor* there!
2 When you enter our supermarket, please take a ....
3 The best stores here are ....
4 Do you need money? The nearest .... is opposite the bus station.
5 Let's meet at the .... where they sell peaches.
6 We asked the .... where to find the sports department.

★ (3) Match these words to the definitions (1–6).

bargain	change	customer
line	products	~~sale~~

1 This is a special time when store prices are cheaper. *sale*
2 This is the name for the things we buy in stores. ....
3 This is the money you get back if you pay too much. ....
4 This is when you buy something good at a very low price. ....
5 This is the name for the person who wants to buy something. ....
6 This is where you have to wait when there are a lot of people who want to do the same thing. ....

Vocabulary page 106

★★ (4) Complete the text with these words.

~~ATM~~	bills	change	coin
line	market stand	price	vendor

At about 11 o'clock, he stopped at an ¹*ATM* to get some money. He had to wait in ² .... for a while. Then he put the ³ .... in his wallet. Next, he went to a ⁴ .... where they were selling shoes. But he didn't buy any. The ⁵ .... didn't look very happy. Maybe there was a problem with the ⁶ .... A small boy near the stand was asking for money. I saw the man give the boy a ⁷ .... Then he went to a café, where he talked on his cell phone. When he finished his coffee, he paid the waiter and left the ⁸ .... on the table.

Reading

Markets or Supermarkets?

At *Shopping Trends* magazine, we asked for our readers' opinions, and here is what they said.

Well, I live in a quiet, small town without many stores, and no market. The nearest market is in the city half an hour away, and there aren't enough buses to get there. So for me, supermarkets are the best option. I can simply park the car and do the shopping. It's more convenient, and there's a greater variety of products than at a market. And markets, for me personally, aren't clean enough.

Sandra

There's a good market near my apartment, so it's easier for me to do my shopping there. Prices are about the same as at the supermarket, but the service is better. I only go to the supermarket when the market is closed.

Trish

I'm a fan of markets— indoor markets or street markets. They're much noisier than supermarkets, but that's all part of the fun! I think the produce is fresher, too. Supermarket fruit, for example, looks good, but doesn't taste good enough for me. Markets are usually a little cheaper too, and always friendlier. The vendors know me, so they know what I want.

Matt

★ **1** Write the correct names.

1 ....clearly prefers markets.

2 .... clearly prefers supermarkets.

3 .... prefers markets, but shops at both.

★ **2** Complete the sentences.

1 There isn't a *market* where Sandra lives.

2 Trish likes the .... she gets at the market.

3 Matt prefers the .... food they sell in markets.

4 Trish goes to the supermarket when the market is ....

5 Matt likes markets because they are .... and friendlier.

★★ **3** Choose the correct option.

1 Sandra / Matt thinks markets are a little dirty.

2 *Trish / Matt* prefers the fruit from markets.

3 *Sandra / Trish* thinks that prices are very similar.

4 *Trish / Matt* knows that supermarkets are quieter places to shop in.

5 *Sandra / Matt* doesn't have a market near her/his home.

6 *Sandra / Trish* can't always get to the market when it's open.

Grammar • Comparatives and superlatives

★ 1 Put the words in the correct order.

1 sister's / is / mine / comfortable / My / than / room / more
My sister's room is more comfortable than mine.

2 town / are / the / beach / The / nearer / our / mountains / than / to

....
....

3 store / in / is / the / town / Benson's / cheapest

....
....

4 market stand / best / has / This / the / products

....
....

5 world / popular / the / The / most / Internet / market / the / is / in

....
....

6 bargains / supermarket / The / has / than / our / stores / better / local

....
....

★★ 2 Complete the text with the correct form of the adjectives.

My parents say it's important to save money when we buy things. Clothes and shoes are often ¹ *cheaper* (cheap) in the street market, but regular stores usually have ² .... (good) quality. The local department store always has the ³ .... (good) selection, but it's also the ⁴ .... (expensive) store in town! However, they have the ⁵ .... (popular) sales too, because you can find really good bargains there. My friends say it's ⁶ .... (easy) to do all the shopping in one big store, but I say it's ⁷ .... (interesting) to visit different places and compare prices and quality.

★★ 3 Write sentences. Use the information in the table.

	Todds	Ekomart	Breezer
Distance from downtown	0.5 km	1.5 km	4 km
Service (good)	★★	★★★	★
Salespeople (friendly)	★	★★	★★★
Prices (expensive)	★★★	★★	★

(* = minimum)

1 Ekomart / Todds / distance
Ekomart is farther from downtown than Todds.

2 Ekomart / Todds / service

....

3 Breezer / Todds / service

....

4 Ekomart / Todds / salespeople

....

5 Ekomart / Breezer / prices

....

6 Breezer / distance
Breezer is the farthest from downtown.

7 Todds / prices

....

• *Too* and *enough*

★ 4 Complete the conversation with *too* or *enough*.

A Do you want to go swimming?

B Not really! It's ¹ *too* cold today. How about going to the movies?

A I can't. I don't have ² .... money.

B Then let's go biking!

A I'm ³ .... tired! I played soccer all afternoon yesterday. What did you do?

B My homework. I didn't have ⁴ .... time to do anything else.

A OK! Was that your math homework?

B Yes, it was.

A Great! So you can help me with mine. I tried, but it was ⁵ .... difficult.

B I'm not sure about that. Your problem is that you don't have ⁶ .... patience!

★★ (5) Kelly doesn't want to go to Dylan's party. Write sentences using *too* or *enough*.

Sorry, Dylan, but …

1 party / end / late.
the party ends too late.

2 I / busy / at home

....
....

3 I / not have / time

....
....

4 your apartment / far / my house

....
....

5 bus / not stop / near

....
....

6 I / not have / money / buy / a present

....
....

7 party dress / not new

....
....

8 I / tired

....
....

Vocabulary • Money verbs

★ (1) Match the sentence beginnings (1–5) to the endings (a–e).

1 Good morning! I'd like to borrow
2 How would you like to pay
3 Excuse me! Do these cost
4 Teri's family is going to sell
5 I always pay for gas

a $6.50 or $8.50?
b by credit card.
c their house.
d for your new suit?
e some money for a Porsche.

★ (2) Complete the advertisements with these verbs.

| afford | lend | pay in cash | ~~Buy~~ | Save | Win |

1 *Buy* 2, get 1 free!

2 .... HUNDREDS of prizes in our new competition!

3 .... $50 *with our special offers!*

4 Best prices in town for your old cell phones! We ....!

Do you need money urgently? We .... instant cash! ASK INSIDE.

WINTER SALES … AT PRICES YOU CAN .... !

★★ (3) Choose the correct options.

1 Did you know? Your brother *won* / *earned* a new bicycle in a competition!
2 Tamara needed money for the trip, so I *borrowed* / *lent* her $50.
3 She *bought* / *cost* her mother a new watch for her birthday.
4 Ellen *paid* / *sold* her old laptop for $40.
5 It wasn't very expensive, so we *afforded* / *paid in cash*.
6 The new store was fantastic! I *earned* / *spent* $80 on T-shirts for my friends.

★★ (4) Complete the text with these verbs.

| afford | borrowed | ~~cost~~ | earned | paid by credit card | saved |

Paula wanted a new smart phone, but it [1] *cost* $500, and she couldn't [2] .... it. She [3] .... the money from her birthday presents, she [4] .... some extra money by doing some work for the neighbors, and she [5] .... the last $50 from her mother. Finally, she and her mother went to the store, and her mother [6] .... Paula's mother says it's better to do that because sometimes there are problems with the products you buy.

Grammar Reference pages 90–91

Vocabulary page 106

Chatroom Asking for help

Speaking and Listening

★ **1** **Match the questions (1–6) to the answers (a–f). Then listen and check.**

11

1 Could you give me change for the coffee machine ?   c
2 Would you mind taking a photo for us?
3 Can you pass me the sugar?
4 Could you give me a hand with these boxes?
5 Would you mind driving me to the station?
6 Could you mail this letter for me?

a Sorry, I can't. I don't drive.
b Sure. Do you want a spoon, too?
c Sorry, I can't. I only have bills.
d OK. There's a post office next to my school.
e No problem. Where are you going to stand?
f Sorry, I can't. I have a pain in my back.

★ **2** **Put the conversation in the correct order. Then listen and check.**

12

a Good idea! Can you get them? They're too high for me.   ....
b I think so. Would you mind paying for this?   ....
c What about some of those snacks?   ....
d Sorry, I can't. I don't have any cash.   ....
e What else do we need for the party?   1.
f Sure. Is that everything?   ....

★ **3** **Complete the conversation with these words. Then listen and check.**

13

| ~~Can~~ | Could | give | mind | problem | Sorry |

Lucy	Olivia!
Olivia	What?
Lucy	¹ *Can* you help me choose a camera? I don't know which one to buy.
Olivia	OK. What kind do you prefer?
Lucy	I want one I can use in the swimming pool.
Olivia	I don't know about those! Let's ask the salesperson. Excuse me! ² .... you show us some cameras for taking pictures underwater?
Salesperson	No ³ .... ! This one is very popular.
Lucy	Would you ⁴ .... taking a photo for us?
Salesperson	⁵ .... , I can't. You have to buy the camera first!
Lucy	What do you think, Olivia?
Olivia	It's your money!
Lucy	OK, I'll buy it. Can you ⁶ .... me a hand with these bags? I need to find my money.
Olivia	Sure!

★★ **4** **Listen to the conversation in Exercise 3 again. Complete the sentences with one word.**

13

1 Lucy wants to *buy* a new camera.
2 She asks Olivia to .... her choose one.
3 They decide to ask the ....
4 They also ask her to .... a photo for them.
5 But the salesperson says that's not ....
6 In the end, Lucy .... to buy the camera.

★★ **5** **Write a conversation. Use phrases from Exercises 1–3 and this information:**

You are shopping for clothes with a friend. Ask your friend to help you decide on three different items. Remember to include your friend's replies.

Speaking and Listening page 115

Grammar • Much, many, a lot of

★ **1** Match the pictures (A–F) to the sentences (1–6).

1 He has a lot of pets.   *E*
2 She has too much furniture.
3 She doesn't have much furniture.
4 He has too many pets.
5 He doesn't have many pets.
6 She has a lot of furniture.

★ **2** Choose the correct options.

1 How *much / many* movie theaters are there in this town?
2 There are a *lot of / much* people waiting in line.
3 There aren't *much / many* good movies to watch this week.
4 We don't have *much / many* time before the movie starts.
5 How *much / many* money do we need?
6 Don't take *a lot of / too many* food with you!

★★ **3** Write sentences with *too much* and *too many*.

1 She / have / old toys / her room
   She has too many old toys in her room.
2 Our parents think / my sister / spend / time / on the phone
   ....
   ....
3 My mother says / I / spend / money / on shoes
   ....
   ....
4 I think my friends / spend / time / on the Internet
   ....
   ....
5 My brother says / I have / hobbies
   ....
   ....
6 There / be / salt / in the soup!
   ....
   ....

★★ **4** Complete the conversation with these words and phrases.

How many	~~How much~~	many	much
too many	too much		

A Those shoes are nice! [1] *How much* did they cost?
B They were on sale for $49.50!
A You were lucky! I didn't see [2] .... shoes I liked.
B What about your shirt? Is that also new?
A Yes! Do you like it? It didn't cost [3] .... ! Only about $10.
B Really? [4] .... did you buy?
A I bought four!
B Wow! I wanted to buy more shoes, but my mom says I have [5] .... shoes already.
A My mom says I spend [6] .... money on clothes, too. But if it's birthday money, I can spend it on whatever I want!

Grammar Reference pages 90–91

Reading

1 **Read the text quickly. Match the headings (1–3) to the paragraphs (A–C).**

1 How do we recognize a shopaholic?
2 What can we do about it?
3 What exactly is the problem?

Too Much Shopping?

A ....
Some people can never get enough of shopping. They're called shopaholics, and they spend their weekends looking for bargains in shopping malls. You can often hear them comparing prices and products. But for many families, this can become a serious problem. There's often a nasty surprise at the end of the month because there isn't enough money to pay for everything.

B ....
There are many ways to discover a shopaholic. Look at their room: are there too many new things in it? Check their planner: how often do they do unnecessary shopping? Look in the garage for unopened boxes of bargains from the stores. Are they spending too much money with their credit card? If you're not sure, ask a friend for their opinion. Friends often see the situation better than we do.

C ....
A lot of people say being patient is more important than being angry. We need to help shopaholics. One of the best ideas is to offer alternatives. Help them to get interested in hobbies. Take them to the movies, theaters or concerts. Ask family and friends to give you a hand. And the next time you go shopping with them, ask them: do you really need this, or is it better for you to save the money for something more important?

2 **Are the statements true (T) or false (F)?**

1 A shopaholic is a person who spends too much time shopping. *T*
2 Shopaholics don't usually spend much money. ....
3 Inviting a shopaholic to a dance class would be a good idea. ....
4 It's a good idea to be angry with shopaholics. ....
5 We don't need to think much before we go shopping. ....

Listening

1 **Listen to four radio advertisements. Number the advertisements in the order you hear them.**
14

a a chance to win a prize ....
b free entry to a club ....
c bargain-price furniture *1*
d tickets by phone ....

2 **Listen again and complete the details.**
14

1 The furniture store closes at *8 p.m.*
2 The date for Mike Springston's concert is
....
3 The bicycle store opens at
....
4 Only ....
customers can get into the club for free.

Brain Trainer

Look at Grammar Reference page 90 and then put *much* and *many* into this sentence.

Too .... people
have too .... money.

Now write the rule.

Writing • A customer review

1 **Read the review. Match the headings (A–D) to the paragraphs (1–4).**

A What I didn't like about the restaurant   *3*
B My general opinion about the restaurant
C What I liked about the restaurant
D General information about the restaurant

Spanish Restaurants

Pepe's Taberna

"Lighting poor, restaurant noisy"

★★★☆☆   Reviewed 30 June 2014

1 Pepe's Taberna is a Spanish restaurant downtown. It's only five minutes from a bus stop, and it's open six days a week (they close on Mondays), from 12 noon until midnight. There are tables for a maximum of 80 people.

2 We went there for lunch. We ordered a big salad and paella, their special rice dish. There was a good selection of soft drinks. The salad was very fresh, and the rice was tasty. The waiters were friendly and attentive, and the prices were very reasonable.

3 However, I don't think the lighting is very good. It's too dark to see what you're eating. I also found it difficult to chat with my friends because it's a little noisy: the tables are very close together, and you can hear other people's conversations.

4 In my opinion, it's a good place for a quick lunch when you're shopping. But it's not the best place for a romantic dinner!

Visited June 2014

Was this review helpful?   Yes

2 **Read the review again. Add these words to the correct section in column A.**

attentive	~~downtown~~
fresh	friendly
good place for a quick lunch	good selection
noisy	~~noon till midnight~~
not for a romantic dinner	reasonable
six days a week	~~Spanish food~~
tasty	too dark

	A Pepe's Taberna	B My restaurant/café: ....
1 location kind of food/cooking opening times	*downtown* *Spanish food* *noon till midnight*	
2 food and drink prices service		
3 atmosphere		
4 recommendation		

3 **Now think of a restaurant or café you visited recently. Write the name at the top of column B. Then write information and ideas in column B.**

4 **Write a review. Use your ideas and information from Exercises 2 and 3.**

1 ....
....
....
2 ....
....
....
3 ....
....
....
4 ....
....
....

Check Your Progress

Grammar

1 Complete the conversation with the Present simple or Present continuous form of the verbs.

A Hi, Tom! **0** *Are* (be) you busy?
B Not really. I **1**........................ (check) my email, that's all.
A Anything interesting?
B One of my friends **2**........................ (want) me to help him paint his room.
A Where **3**........................ (he/live)?
B It's about twenty minutes by bus. But he has a swimming pool!
A That sounds OK, if you **4**........................ (not mind) the work.
B So what **5**........................ (you/do) now?
A I **6**........................ (wait) for Angela. I have to talk to her.

/ 6 points

2 Complete the text with the Past simple or Past continuous form of the verbs.

Hi Mandy!
How are you? **0** *Did you have* (you/have) a good weekend? I have to tell you what **1**........................ (happen) yesterday! Kev and I were in that new mall near the park. We **2**........................ (look) for some running shoes on sale, when we **3**........................ (see) some really nice ones in a store window. The salesperson **4**........................ (bring) them out, and Kev **5**........................ (try) them on when this boy **6**........................ (take) Kev's old shoes and ran away! Amazing! Kev had to buy the new shoes anyway, and I **7**........................ (feel) sorry for him because they weren't cheap.
Write soon,
Amy

/ 7 points

3 Choose the correct options.

0 Tom loves .... cards, but I prefer video games!
  a play   **(b)** playing   **c** when play
1 Ana always gets better grades .... Albert.
  a that   **b** than   **c** to
2 Their car is old-fashioned; our car is much .... !
  a most modern
  b more modern
  c least modern
3 He's .... boy in the world.
  a the happier   **b** happiest   **c** the happiest
4 Rita bought .... jacket in the store!
  a the most expensive
  b too expensive
  c the more expensive
5 Marta is .... excited about the trip. She can't sleep!
  a enough   **b** too   **c** much
6 I'd love to buy the coat, but I don't have .... money!
  a many   **b** too   **c** enough
7 Tammie doesn't mind waiting! She has .... time.
  a a lot of   **b** much   **c** many

/ 7 points

Vocabulary

4 Choose the correct options.

0 Excuse me! How much does this .... ?
  a buy   **b** price   **(c)** cost
1 You can leave your bags on the .... at the top of the stairs.
  a yard   **b** patio   **c** landing
2 Front desk? There's no .... on my bed!
  a mirror   **b** pillow   **c** rug
3 My parents keep a lot of old stuff down in the .... .
  a ceiling   **b** basement   **c** roof

4 Paul isn't very .... insects, but I think they're really fascinating!
  a interested in   **b** good at   **c** tired of

5 This photo isn't at all clear—it's .... .
  a colorful   **b** dramatic   **c** blurry

6 The difference between the two parts of the photo is unreal. I think it's .... .
  a boring   **b** fake   **c** horrible

7 Jake doesn't have many friends. I feel .... him.
  a proud of
  b excited about
  c sorry for

8 Excuse me! The .... to pay for things is over there!
  a line   **b** ATM   **c** customer

9 There's a street market in town today! Let's see if we can find a .... .
  a coin   **b** bargain   **c** salesperson

10 I'd love to buy these shoes, but I can't .... them.
  a cost   **b** save   **c** afford

/ 10 points

Speaking

5 Complete the conversations with these words and phrases.

| a little | Can you | give me a hand |
| like | ~~No problem~~ | Would you mind |

A Can I ask you something?
B ⁰ *No problem.*
A Could you ¹ .... with these boxes?
B Sure! Where do you want them?
A I need to take them up to the attic.
B An attic? There's no attic in my apartment! What's it ² .... ?
A Nothing special! There aren't any windows, so it's ³ .... dark. ⁴ .... opening the door first?
B No problem. Is it up these stairs?
A That's right.
B ⁵ .... go first then? I don't know the way.
A OK!

| can | I don't | I'm sorry | Is it OK | mind if |

A Dad! ⁶ .... if we play soccer in the backyard?
B All six of you? No, ⁷ .... The yard isn't big enough!
A Instead, ⁸ .... we play music in the garage?
B Yes, that's all right, but I'll take the car out first.
A Do you ⁹ .... we get some pizza for dinner?
B No, ¹⁰ .... But you better clean up the kitchen when you finish!

/ 10 points

Translation

6 Translate the sentences.

1 I don't have enough money to buy the CD.
....

2 Could you tell me where the nearest ATM is?
....

3 That store sells the tastiest sandwiches in town!
....

4 Can I borrow $20 to go to the street market?
....

5 I was going home on the bus when she called me.
....

/ 5 points

Dictation

7 Listen and write.

15

1 ....
2 ....
3 ....
4 ....
5 ....

/ 5 points

In the News

Vocabulary • News and media

★ (1) **Label the pictures with these words and *news*.**

| anchor | flash | international | ~~local~~ |
| national | paper | website | |

1 *local news*
2 ....
3 ....
4 ....
5 ....
6 ....
7 ....

★ (2) **Match these words to the definitions (1–7).**

| blog | current affairs show | headline |
| ~~interview~~ | journalist | podcast | report |

1 When one person asks someone else a lot of questions.   *interview*
2 Personal news and comments from an individual on a webpage.   ....
3 This is the person who finds and presents information for a newspaper.   ....
4 This is the name for the information which they present.   ....
5 This is the title for a newspaper story.

   ....
6 News in the form of audio files for downloading from the Internet.   ....
7 Where people present and comment on events in the news.   ....

★ (3) **Match the sentence beginnings (1–8) to the endings (a–h).**

1 My sister loves clothes   *e*
2 I don't know all the details
3 We heard about a tsunami
4 She often uses her smart phone
5 My father always reads news stories
6 Opinion articles are not the same
7 I love our local newspaper
8 Sean has no time to read newspapers,

a but he often listens to podcasts.
b written by the same journalist.
c to access a news website.
d because I recognize people and places in it.
e and reads a fashion blog every week.
f on a news flash this morning.
g because I only read the headlines.
h as serious news reports.

★★ (4) **Put the letters in the correct order to complete the text.**

I don't mind watching the news on TV, like my parents, but I'm not interested in those [1] *current affairs* (truncer frasifa) shows, where the news [2] .... (crnaho) introduces a topic and then [3] .... (winevestir) people who know more about it. And then they all give their opinions. I only look at the newspaper for the football, but my uncle's a [4] .... (jolisaturn), and he says I should read the [5] .... (delihsane), and then the full [6] .... (perrot) if I want to. But it's easier for me to access a news [7] .... (ebistew): they have the news in pictures, on video and in podcasts, too. And the best part is the [8] .... (globs), because you can always find one on a topic you like.

Vocabulary page 107

Reading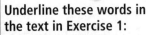

★ **1** Read the texts quickly and match the people (1–3) to their news priorities (a–c).

1 Emily
2 her brother
3 her parents

a current affairs
b pop culture
c sports

★ **2** Match the phrases (1–6) to the blanks (a–f) in the text.

1 on his cell phone, too
2 blogs if they have them
3 you can't even talk to them
4 just a few things
5 that's boring for us
6 Billy reads that regularly, too

★ **3** Are the statements true (T) or false (F)?

1 Emily prefers cartoons to news. *T*
2 Her parents are only interested in the news on weekends. ....
3 Her brother buys a special sports magazine. ....
4 Billy follows his friend's news from New Delhi. ....
5 Emily enjoys reading a friend's blog. ....

Interview with EMILY

We asked Emily to tell us how her family get their news. This is what she said.

My mom and dad are still kind of traditional. They've always watched the news on TV at lunchtime. I mean, a *5..* , because we can't watch the cartoons on the other channel. Plus, on the weekends, they've always bought the Sunday newspapers. Then they spend half the morning reading them, so b .... !

My older brother Billy is studying biology in college, and he's always been into sports, like tennis, biking and swimming. He gets all his sports news from a specialized website, and on the weekends he gets updates on the tennis c .... . Oh, and his best friend from school is living abroad and has started a blog on life in New Delhi. So d .... .

As for me, I'm in my last year of high school. I've never been interested in the news, such as current affairs shows. I've hardly ever watched it on TV, except for e .... , like the September 11 attacks. What's important to me are my favorite singers and actors, so I follow them on the social networks, and f .... . I also started my own blog at school, so we can all keep in touch next year if we want to.

Grammar • Present perfect

★ 1 Match the sentence beginnings (1–6) to the endings (a–f).

1 I've been to Mexico,
2 She's had that toy
3 We've had
4 Have you ever
5 What have you
6 Where have you

a been all afternoon?
b seen on TV recently?
c had a bad dream?
d some very bad weather recently.
e since she was five.
f but I've never been to Brazil.

★ 2 Complete the first lines of newspaper reports with the correct form of these verbs.

| appear | arrive | discover | ~~escape~~ |
| interview | open | present | record |

1 A gray-haired monkey has *escaped* from the zoo.

2 A local student has .... a podcast at the radio station.

3 The mayor has .... the new theme park in the city.

4 The high school drama club has .... on the national news.

5 An American journalist has .... an award to the city.

6 Local history teachers have .... a Native American boat in the river.

7 A local student has .... Katy Perry about her new album.

8 25 Swedish students have .... in town on an exchange visit.

★ 3 Complete the questions with the Present perfect form of these verbs. Then add the correct verb in the answers.

1 *Have you ever climbed* (you/ever climb) a volcano? No, I *haven't*.
2 .... (your brother/ever do) the housework? No, he ....
3 .... (your parents/ever travel) to the US? No, they ....
4 .... (your family/ever visit) Paris? Yes, they ....
5 .... (you/ever buy) an expensive present? Yes, I ....
6 .... (your friend/ever lose) her cell phone? Yes, she ....

★ 4 Put the words in the correct order.

1 the US / wanted / Pablo / has / to / visit / always
   Pablo has always wanted to visit the US.
2 written / you / English / ever / someone / to / Have / in / ?
   ....
   ....
3 interested / comics / always / in / has / Paul / been
   ....
   ....
4 the / have / camping / weekend / gone / often / on / We
   ....
   ....
5 tried / a / Have / face / draw / you / person's / ever / to / ?
   ....
   ....
6 gone / parents / without / Have / vacation / your / ever / on / you / ?
   ....
   ....
7 been / on / your / ever / family / Has / TV / ?
   ....
   ....
8 championship / Has / a / team / ever / your / football / won / national / ?
   ....
   ....

Vocabulary • Adverbs of manner

★ **5** Complete the conversation with the correct form of the verbs.

A Why don't you write a report for our school blog?

B Me? I ¹ *'ve never written* (never/write) a report in my life!

A Not even in English class?

B I don't think so!

A ² .... (you/ever interview) someone?

B No. I'm not a journalist! Have you?

A Yes, I ³ .... (interview) three or four people.

B And how many reports ⁴ .... (you/do)?

A Three.

B Well, you would have to help me, then. ⁵ .... (you/think) about a person to interview?

A The school bus driver must have some interesting stories!

B OK. I'll think of the questions. Can you show me how to organize the report?

A Sure! I ⁶ .... (prepare) that for you already. Here you are!

★ **1** Match the questions (1–5) to the answers (a–e).

1 Does Carlos write well?   *d*
2 How fast can you run?
3 Do your friends work hard?
4 Could you speak more slowly, please?
5 How early do you want to leave?

a Sorry, I didn't realize I was speaking so fast.
b Yes, they do. Very hard!
c About 7 a.m., so we don't get there late!
d I think he writes very clearly.
e I can do a kilometer in ten minutes!

★ **2** Complete the sentences with the opposite adverb.

1 Jim plays the guitar well, but he sings *badly*.
2 She always drives carefully, but last night she drove ....
3 The children played happily on the floor, but their mother looked .... at the newspaper.
4 Magda reads fast in her own language, but she reads .... in English.
5 I like to get home early, but sometimes the bus is ....!
6 Mom! Don't talk so loudly on the phone! We're trying to work .... in our room.

★ **3** Choose the correct options.

A So, Alan. What's it like to be a blog writer?

B It's a lot of fun! I can be sitting ¹ *carelessly /* quietly at the computer when my cell phone rings ² *slowly / loudly,* and it's a friend with a good idea for a story. So I check the details ³ *early / carefully* and then upload my comments. I don't like to work too ⁴ *fast / angrily* because that's when I make mistakes.

A Do a lot of people write back?

B It depends, really. Sometimes I can wait ⁵ *patiently / sadly* at the computer and nothing happens. Other times people will ⁶ *happily / late* upload a dozen comments in ten minutes!

★★ **4** Complete the text with the adverb form of the words.

I was waiting ¹ *patiently* (patient) for a bus the other day when a dog appeared and started barking ² .... (loud). I'm usually a little scared of dogs, and there was no one else around. I thought ³ .... (hard) for a moment and remembered I had a cracker in my pocket. So I took it out ⁴ .... (careful) and gave it to the dog. It stopped barking immediately and wagged its tail ⁵ .... (happy). Then I touched it and talked to it, and ⁶ .... (slow) we became friends. The dog's been at my house now for three weeks!

Grammar Reference pages 92–93

Vocabulary page 107

Speaking and Listening

★ **1** Choose the correct options. Then listen and check.

16
1 **A** I just saw Matt Damon at the airport!
   B *Come on now! / You're kidding!*
   A Oh yeah? Turn on the TV!

2 **A** Have you heard the news?
   B What?
   A The Yankees won the World Series!
   B *That's impossible! / Go ahead!* They lost most of their games last year!

3 **A** Hey! Our history teacher has written a book!
   B *I don't mind. / I don't believe it!*
   A She has! There's a copy in the library.

4 **A** Hi, guys! Have you seen this?
   B What is it?
   A An autograph from Cristiano Ronaldo.
   B *No problem! / No! Really?*
   A It is! My cousin works at the stadium.

5 **A** Awesome! We have a day off tomorrow!
   B *That's strange! / That's a shame!* Tomorrow's Wednesday. Why don't you check the calendar?

6 **A** Have you read the paper?
   B What happened?
   A They're closing the local gym!
   B *I'd like that! / That's ridiculous!* They only opened it last year!

★ **2** Put the sentences in the correct order. Then listen and check.

17
a What news?   ....
b No, I'm not! Look, here's a photo!   ....
c Why not?   ....
d Have you heard the news?   *1*
e Yes, but it says they can't sell them.   ....
f Because they don't have enough factories to build them!   ....
g You're kidding!   ....
h They've invented a car that runs on hydrogen!   ....

★ **3** Complete the conversation with these phrases. Then listen and check.

18

| Are you sure | I don't believe it | ~~something scary~~ |
| strange lights | that's not all | the best part |

A Have you seen this story about a camel?
B No! What happened?
A This tourist was driving along when he saw [1]*something scary* on the road ahead, and made an emergency stop.
B So? That sounds normal!
A In the desert, in the middle of the night? There were [2]........................ moving, too!
B No! Really?
A Yes, but [3]........................ ! He thought it was an alien from space!
B You're kidding!
A No, I'm not. That's what it says here. So he called the police.
B [4]........................ !
A Yes, but you haven't heard [5]........................ yet!
B What's that?
A They told him that police sometimes put reflectors on camels in order to prevent traffic accidents!
B Amazing! [6]........................ that's a real story?!

★★ **4** Listen to the conversation in Exercise 3 again. Are the statements true (T) or false (F)?

18
1 The driver was a local man.   *F*
2 The story took place in a desert.   ....
3 He was very confused about what he saw.   ....
4 He called his wife.   ....
5 The police explained the strange phenomenon. ....

★★ **5** Write a conversation. Use expressions from Exercises 1–3 and this information:

You tell a friend an amazing story you heard on TV. Your friend isn't sure if the story is real. Remember to include your friend's responses.

Speaking and Listening page 116

Grammar • Present perfect vs Past simple

★ **1** Match the beginnings of the news reports (1–5) to the endings (a–e).

1 A cat has attacked a large dog.   *d*
2 The high school's website has reached 5,000 visits.
3 A local girl has won a national blog-writing contest.
4 High school students have recorded a podcast for the city council.
5 The local newspaper has introduced a news section for teenagers.

a The school's principal said last year's maximum was only 2,400 visits.
b The paper said the section was requested by teens.
c They made the recording in English for tourists.
d When the cat found itself in a corner, it jumped on the dog.
e Elena Marquez won first prize for her fashion blog last weekend.

Girl wins national blog contest.

★ **2** Choose the correct options.

1 Steve *has broken* / (broke) his arm last weekend.
2 Oh no! My car *has disappeared* / *disappeared!*
3 Firefighters *have rescued* / *rescued* three people from an elevator yesterday.
4 My grandmother *has had* / *had* two operations.
5 A teenager *has won* / *won* this year's national chess contest.
6 Five thousand people *have attended* / *attended* the local music festival.
7 We *have lost* / *lost* our suitcases twice this year.
8 A young woman *has had* / *had* a baby in a taxi last night.

★★ **3** Write the correct form of the verbs.

A What's the most amazing newspaper story ¹*you've ever read* (you/ever read)?
B I ² .... (not read) very many, but I ³ .... (hear) a lot of stories from other people!
A For example?
B Well, it's the silly ones I remember the best. A player ⁴ .... (have) to stay in the hospital with head injuries after a golf game.
A What happened?
B He ⁵ .... (hit) the ball really hard, the ball ⁶ .... (go) up into the sky and ⁷ .... (kill) a passing duck.
A You're kidding!
B No, no! And then the duck ⁸ .... (fall) out of the sky and ⁹ .... (strike) the player on the head!
A I don't believe it! That's the most amazing story anyone ¹⁰ .... (ever tell) me!
B Imagine that!

★★ **4** Complete the text with the correct form of these verbs.

receive	recommend	say	send
start	take	~~win~~	write

Local Teen Wins National Blog Contest

Elena Marquez, a 15-year-old from GBS High School, ¹*won* first prize in a national contest for school blogs. Elena ² .... writing the blog two years ago when she ³ .... a camera as a present. She ⁴ .... over a thousand photos of teenagers in the street, and she ⁵ .... a fashion report every month. Her design teacher at school ⁶ .... that she enter the contest, and the organizers ⁷ .... her a text message last Monday to tell her about the prize. Her family ⁸ .... they were very proud of her.

Grammar Reference pages 92–93

Reading

1 **Read the text quickly and choose the best headline.**

a Amusing Pet Monkeys
b Humans Versus Monkeys
c Winemaking in South Africa

AnimalNews.netcom

HOME   NEWS   BLOG   FEATURES   PHOTOS

....

by Wayne Chapman

There are many stories about conflicts between people and wild animals. We have heard about elephants in Africa eating village people's plants. There have also been reports of coyotes coming into people's yards in the US. As towns and cities use more and more land, animals have less land to live on. Usually the animals lose the competition. But in some places, the animals are slowly winning.

I've discovered an amazing story from South Africa. In one part of the country, people grow a lot of grapes for making wine. A few years ago, they began to have problems with large groups of monkeys which live in the mountains nearby. The monkeys love the sweet fruit. They ate all the grapes they wanted and then ran off to the mountains to sleep. The farmers reacted angrily, but some people defended the monkeys. "The monkeys have always lived here," they said.

But recently, the monkeys have become difficult because they get into people's homes to steal food. And they're not friendly like the monkeys on TV! One day, they even frightened a ten-year-old boy when he heard strange noises in the kitchen. People call the police, but they're not allowed to hurt the animals. So now, many families are tired of the monkeys and are selling their homes and moving away.

Imagine that! If you have any good animal stories from your town or city, please send them to me!

2 **Complete the sentences with a word from the text.**

1 Wild animals living near human beings often create *conflicts*.
2 The problem is often that people use more and more ....
3 The monkeys in South Africa enjoy eating ....
4 The farmers were very .... with the monkeys.
5 Now the monkeys are more ....
6 Many people are .... of the monkeys, and sell their homes.

Listening

1 **Listen to the interview and choose the best answer.**

19

The main subject of the interview is Steve Black's .... .
a preferences in music
b career as a musician
c concert performances

2 **Listen again and choose the correct option.**

19

1 Steve Black plays the *guitar* / *drums*.
2 His parents *played* / *didn't play* a lot of music.
3 When he was in school, he was a *good* / *bad* student.
4 He *writes* / *doesn't write* most of the lyrics.
5 His group has recorded *six* / *sixteen* albums.

Writing • A profile

1 Find and correct the mistakes in these phrases. (S= spelling, G= grammar, P= punctuation)

1 wining tenis titles, and he turned proffesional at fifteen (S)

winning tennis titles, and he turned professional

2 he did not lose his ability (G)

....

3 in 2008 he has also started a foundation (G)

....

4 which is one of the balearic islands in spain (P)

....

2 Read the text. Match the phrases (1–4) from Exercise 1 to the blanks (a–d).

Rafael Nadal is one of the greatest tennis players of all time. He was the first player to win the French Open seven times, and he is currently No. 2 in the world. I admire him for his skill and his character, and also for the work he does through his foundation.

Nadal was born in 1986 on the island of Mallorca, ª .4. . He went to school in his hometown of Manacor. At the age of 12, he was already ᵇ .... . He did not move to Barcelona to train, but stayed in Manacor in order to finish school. In 2005, at the age of 19, he won his first French Open title.

He continues playing tennis and winning tournaments, but ᶜ .... to help children and young people locally and abroad. In 2010 he visited different educational projects in India to show his support for the projects and help other people become aware of them. Nadal has become internationally famous, but ᵈ .... to understand and help other people.

3 Put these ideas in column A, according to the paragraph they appear in.

achievements	career	conclusion
early life	education	~~introduction~~
recent activities	reasons for admiring	

	A Rafael Nadal's profile	B .... profile
Paragraph 1	*introduction*	
Paragraph 2		
Paragraph 3		

4 Think of a person you would like to write about. Add information about that person to column B.

5 Write a profile of the person you have chosen in three paragraphs. Use your ideas and information from Exercises 3 and 4.

....
....
....
....
....
....
....
....
....
....
....
....

Enjoy Your Vacation!

Vocabulary • Vacation

★ **1** **Match the sentence beginnings (1–7) to the endings (a–g).**

1 Do you eat out on vacation,   *e*
2 I prefer to stay in hotels,
3 We like to go camping
4 I've only seen a few sights
5 Do you often take trips
6 We got lost in the city
7 She's written a travel blog

a or do you prefer to vacation at home?
b and we don't mind what the weather's like.
c and had to take a taxi back.
d about her trip to Turkey.
e or do you cook in the apartment?
f because many of them are closed.
g but I can't usually afford to.

★★ **2** **Complete the sentences with the correct form of these verbs.**

book	buy	check into	get
<s>lose</s>	pack	put up	

1 Good morning! Unfortunately, they've *lost* our luggage!
2 The weather was cold and cloudy, so he didn't .... a tan.
3 Dad, you should learn how to .... a tent before going on vacation!
4 Have you .... your bags for the trip?
5 Our neighbors have .... a two-week hotel stay in Portugal.
6 We .... the hotel and then went out for a walk.
7 How many souvenirs have you .... ?

★★ **3** **Choose the correct options.**

1 Jorge and Maria *went /(booked)* a resort in the Caribbean.
2 They didn't usually *take / go* a trip, but this year was different.
3 They *put up / packed* their bags at home.
4 They had a good flight, but they *got lost / lost* their luggage.
5 So they didn't *go / get* sightseeing when they arrived.
6 Instead of *staying / buying* souvenirs, they had to *stay / buy* clothes!

★★ **4** **Complete the conversation with these words**

hotel	hotel	luggage	sightseeing
<s>souvenirs</s>	tan	tent	

A So what was Miami like?
B Wonderful!
A Did you buy any ¹*souvenirs*?
B Just a few things for the family.
A Did you book the ²........................ , or did you look for a room when you arrived?
B We went without a hotel reservation. The idea was to go camping, but there was no place to put up a ³........................ .
A What about the campgrounds?
B They were too crowded.
A So what did you do?
B We checked into a cheap ⁴........................ and stayed there.
A Did you go ⁵........................ ?
B Not really! We just went to the beach and got a good ⁶........................ .
A Yes, I noticed! So you had a good time?
B Yes, except that Derek lost his ⁷........................ on the way home!
A What a shame!

Vocabulary page 108

Reading

★ **(1)** **Read the texts quickly and choose the best title.**

   a Your Adventure Vacation

   b Your Cheap Vacation

   c Your Family Vacation

Madison

In my family, we've been to the beach every summer since I was little. It's always been fun because we live in a big city and the change is great! I love staying in a hotel because I don't have to make the bed, and we love eating out because my parents don't have to cook, and I don't have to do the dishes afterward! And we all enjoy getting a good tan. But the best of all is that my parents pay for the vacation!

Noah

There are six of us in our family, so we've often had problems with vacations. But for the last five years, we've agreed together on where we want to go. Last year we booked a flight to Chicago. Then when we got there, we decided to have time to go sightseeing in the city, time to go shopping for souvenirs and then free time for different activities. That way, we avoid a lot of silly arguments!

We're twin brothers, and we've gone on a lot of different vacations with our parents. We've usually enjoyed them too, except for museums and monuments, which are a little boring. So this year, because we're already 16, our parents let us go camping with some friends, and it was awesome. We did a lot of walking and climbing, we didn't get lost, and it wasn't expensive.

Rob and Doug

★ **(2)** **Complete the sentences with the correct names.**

1 *Noah* flew to Chicago last year.

2 .... had a new kind of vacation this year.

3 .... usually goes to the beach.

4 .... didn't go with the family this year.

5 .... often goes to a hotel.

6 ....'s family organizes the way they spend their time.

★★ **(3)** **Are the statements true (T) or false (F)?**

1 Madison lives in a small town.   *F*

2 She often does chores at home.   ....

3 Noah's family can't always agree on what to do.   ....

4 They had a lot of arguments last year.   ....

5 The twins aren't very interested in museums and monuments.   ....

6 They had a pretty lazy vacation this year.   ....

Brain Trainer

Underline these adjectives in the texts in Exercise 1:

boring
silly
expensive
free
awesome
different

Now do Exercise 1.

Grammar • Present perfect + *for* and *since*; *How long?*

★ ① Choose the correct options.

1 We've been here *for* / *since* six days.
2 She's read three books *for* / *since* we arrived.
3 They haven't been camping *for* / *since* 2012.
4 We haven't watched TV *for* / *since* a week!
5 I haven't stayed in a hotel *for* / *since* I was ten!
6 They haven't stopped dancing *for* / *since* three hours!

★ ② Rewrite the sentences. Put *for* or *since* in the correct place.

1 My family has lived here ten years.
  My family has lived here for ten years.
2 I've gone to this school 2012.
  ....
3 Carrie and I have been friends we were kids.
  ....
4 We haven't seen Grandma a long time.
  ....
5 I've wanted a new bicycle six months.
  ....

★★ ③ Complete the conversation with these words.

> | the end of | the last five weeks | the last two |
> |---|---|---|
> | last weekend | three years | ~~your birthday~~ |

A Irene! I haven't seen you since ¹*your birthday* in May! How are you?
B Fine, thanks! And you? Where have you been for ² .... months?
A Oh, I've been traveling, you know. I had an exchange trip to Mexico. I've only been home since ³ ....
B Did you have a good time?
A It was very interesting, yes. I've studied Spanish for ⁴ .... now, so I was able to practice a lot! But what about you? What's new?
B I've been on vacation since ⁵ .... June, when school finished. And I've had a summer job for ⁶ .... , so I'm earning a little money.
A That's wonderful! I'm very happy for you!

★★ ④ Write sentences to complete the postcard.

POSTCA

Hi Jackie!
Here we are in Italy! ¹ *We / be here / ten days*, and it's been great. ² *We / go / beach / every day / we arrived*, and the water's perfect. ³ *My parents / rent a car / five days*, so we're doing some sightseeing as well. I'm writing now from Venice. ⁴ *We / be / in the city / ten o'clock this morning*, and there are more tourists than local people! We're having a drink in a café, and ⁵ *I / write / five postcards / we sat down at the table*. I wanted to write a travel blog, of course, but ⁶ *I / be / too busy / our vacation started*, so you'll have to wait until we get back home before you see the photos. Our vacation has been a little tiring, but ⁷ *I / sleep / very well / we got here*!
Love,
Lucas

1 *We've been here for ten days.*
2 ....
3 ....
4 ....
5 ....
6 ....
7 ....

★ ⑤ Make questions for the <u>underlined</u> answers.

1 I've sent <u>twenty</u> text messages since this morning.
2 She's had her MP3 player <u>since Christmas</u>.
3 He's been on the plane <u>for four hours</u>.
4 They've driven <u>three hundred</u> kilometers today.
5 She hasn't gotten up early <u>for a week</u>!
6 We've been at the beach <u>since two o'clock</u>.

1 *How many text messages have you sent?*
2 ....
3 ....
4 ....
5 ....
6 ....

Grammar Reference pages 94–95

Vocabulary • Meanings of *get*

★ **1** **Match these verbs to the meanings of *get* in the sentences (1–6). Use the correct forms.**

> arrive   buy   ~~bring~~   become   receive   walk

1 Can you get me some milk from the fridge?
   bring

2 I got this new shirt on sale.
   ....

3 What time did you get home after the party?
   ....

4 We got on the bus near the stadium.
   ....

5 When it got dark, we made a fire.
   ....

6 Did you get that watch for your birthday?
   ....

★ **2** **Choose the correct meaning for the verb *get*.**

1 I got a phone call from my friend.
   brought / received

2 We got off the bus across the street from the station.
   arrived at / walked

3 We got to the hotel about three o'clock.
   bought / arrived at

4 It got cold in the room.
   became / brought

5 Room service got some blankets for us.
   brought / bought

6 We got some souvenirs the next morning.
   bought / became

★ **3** **Put the words in the correct order.**

1 **A** this / school / you / get / did / to / morning / How / ?
   How did you get to school this morning?
   B I took the bus.

2 **A** Why did you switch on the light?
   B frightened / the / Because / I / in / got / dark
   ....

3 **A** Have you seen my jacket anywhere?
   B you / moment / Yes, / it / for / in / I'll / a / get
   ....

4 **A** Did you have a good time at the market?
   B new / some / Yes, / I / shoes / got
   ....

5 **A** What happened to your friend?
   B train / He / the / got / disappeared / on / and / !
   ....

6 **A** message / Did / my / get / you / ?
   ....
   B What message? I haven't seen any messages!

★★ **4** **Read the text. Replace *get* with the correct form of these verbs.**

> arrive at   become   buy   bring   receive   ~~walk~~

We ¹ **got** off the train at a small station in the countryside, and walked to the campground. It ² **was getting** dark, and we were tired from the trip. When we ³ **got to** the campsite, it was difficult to see. We had to ⁴ **get** a flashlight from the man in the small corner store at the entrance, and then we went to put up the tent. Half an hour later, we were still trying, but we were lucky because we ⁵ **got** some help from one of the other campers. Then we sent Joe to ⁶ **get** some wood, so we could light a fire.

1 *walked*
2 ....
3 ....
4 ....
5 ....
6 ....

Vocabulary page 108

Chatroom Asking for information

Speaking and Listening

★ 1 **Match the questions (1–6) to the answers (a–f). Then listen and check.**
20

1 Excuse me! Can you help us? *f*
2 Where's a good place to buy souvenirs?
3 Is there a good place to have coffee there?
4 How can we get there?
5 Is it far?
6 How long does it take to get to the bus station?

a It's about a ten-minute walk.
b Yes, there's a nice little café on the corner.
c Not really. It's less than one kilometer.
d There's a good store across from the museum.
e Well, you can walk or take a bus.
f Sure! What are you looking for?

★ 2 **Put the conversation in the correct order. Then listen and check.**
21

a Is it far from here? ....
b Oh, yes! That's next to the church on North Street. ....
c Thanks very much! ....
d Excuse me! Can you help me? *1*. ....
e It's about five minutes down that street over there. ....
f Sure! What's the problem? ....
g I'm looking for a restaurant called Cool Kitchen. ....

★★ 3 **Complete the conversation with these words. Then listen and check.**
22

| ~~a good place~~ | can I get | go down this street |
| How long | on the left | the mall |

A Excuse me! Can you help me?
B Sure! What do you need?
A Is there ¹ *a good place* to buy camera batteries near here?
B There's a camera store on Main Street, but that's a little far away from here.
A ² .... does it take to get there?
B It takes a while if you're walking.
A How about a big grocery store? They usually have batteries.
B OK! Yes, there's one next to ³ .... down the street.
A How ⁴ .... there?
B It's about a ten-minute walk.
A Great!
B OK. Well, ⁵ .... till you see a big church on the corner.
A All right.
B Then cross the intersection ⁶ .... , and the mall's on the other side of the street.
A Perfect! Thanks very much.
B You're welcome!

★★ 4 **Listen to the conversation in Exercise 3 again. Choose the correct options.**
22

1 There are *two* / *three* places to buy camera batteries.
2 Main Street *is* / *isn't* near where the speakers are.
3 The camera store *is* / *isn't* in the mall.
4 The girl *is visiting* / *lives in* the town.
5 The mall is *before* / *after* the intersection.

★★ 5 **Write a conversation. Use phrases from Exercises 1–3 and this information:**

An English-speaking tourist in your hometown asks you about a good place to eat out. You recommend a restaurant and describe its location.

Speaking and Listening page 117

Grammar • Past simple with *just*

★ **1** Match the questions (1–6) to the answers (a–f).

1 What's the matter with Derek?   c
2 Has anyone seen my glasses?
3 Is this the bus for Providence?
4 Did I give you my cell phone?
5 Are those my class notes?
6 Can I speak to Felicity, please?

a Sorry! I just spilled water on them!
b Sorry, she just went out.
c He just lost his luggage.
d I'm sorry, you just missed it.
e You just sat on them, Grandma.
f No! You just put it in your bag!

★ **2** Complete the sentences with the correct form of these verbs.

blow   go   lose   melt   put   ~~use~~

1 Somebody just *used* all the sunscreen!
2 I just .... my hotel key card.
3 The wind just .... my magazine into the pool!
4 We bought ice cream, but it just .... !
5 Lewis just .... up the tent, and there's a coyote coming this way!
6 I just .... shopping and forgot the eggs.

★ **3** Put the words in the correct order.

1 travel / blog / just / London / about / I / wrote / a
   I just wrote a travel blog about London.
2 prize / in / just / a / Liz / a / competition / won
   ....
3 bought / new / dad / just / Jake's / a / car
   ....
4 booked / a / Shane / hotel / just / Germany / in
   ....
5 Colorado / They / came / camping / back / from / in / just
   ....
6 ate / good / just / restaurant / a / very / out / at / We
   ....

★★ **4** Look at the pictures. Write sentences using *just*.

1 *He just fell off his bike.*
2 ....
3 ....
4 ....
5 ....
6 ....

Grammar Reference pages 94–95

Reading

1 **Read the text quickly. What kind of text is it?**

a a magazine article
b a travel blog
c a letter to someone's family

WEDNESDAY We're continuing our week in Amsterdam. Mom and Dad have gone to the Rijksmuseum, and we just returned to the hotel from the Van Gogh Museum. It was modern and interesting. I liked the painting of his shoes, but Clara says the picture of the yellow house is her favorite. We also went to a huge street market where we bought some souvenirs.

THURSDAY We've been up since seven o'clock this morning because we've been on a day trip to visit a real windmill. It was made of wood and was really pretty on the outside, but full of spiders' webs on the inside. It was really old, but it still worked! We had lunch in a little town before coming back to the city. (Did you know the Dutch have mayonnaise with their French fries?!)

And this afternoon we went for a walk in one of the big parks. I've never seen so many flowers!

FRIDAY Tomorrow's our last day here. This morning we went to see Anne Frank's house, because I read the book in school last year, and I wanted to see it for myself. It made me think about how lucky I am. Anyway, we're eating out tonight at an Indonesian restaurant, so tomorrow's blog post will be about exotic food!

2 **Choose the correct options.**

1 The writer *visited* /*didn't visit* the Rijksmuseum.
2 They went shopping on *Wednesday* / *Thursday*.
3 The windmill *was* / *wasn't* very clean inside.
4 On Thursday afternoon, they *left* / *stayed in* the hotel.
5 To the writer, Anne Frank's house was *boring* / *interesting*.

Listening

1 **Listen and choose the correct options.**

23

1 The speaker is going to have *Chinese* / *Indian* / *Italian* food.
2 He and his friend have eaten a lot of *fast food* / *pizza* / *sandwiches* this week.
3 The woman says lunch at the restaurant costs *$6* / *$15* / *$16*.
4 The restaurant is *takeout* / *self-service* / *waiter service*.
5 The woman *explains how to get there* / *shows them the way on a map* / *takes them there herself*.

2 **Who says these phrases? Listen again and write**
23 **B for the boy or W for the woman.**

1 What kind of food   *W*
2 every day this week   ....
3 I've eaten there   ....
4 what's a buffet lunch?   ....
5 you get the food yourself   ....
6 Come with me!   ....

Writing • A travel guide

1 Complete the text with these adjectives.

beautiful	helpful	~~historic~~
musical	popular	sunny

One of my favorite vacation places is the ¹ *historic* city of Williamsburg in eastern Virginia. It's not too big, it has a lot of good stores and restaurants, and the people are friendly and ² .... Spring is the best time to visit, when the weather's bright and ³ .... , and the flowers are in bloom. There are a lot of things to see and do in and around Williamsburg. The Revolutionary City is the most famous and ⁴ .... attraction. You can visit all of it, and it's interactive: you can see people wearing eighteenth-century clothes, hear the ⁵ .... instruments and smell the spices they cooked with. You can even meet the heroes of the American Revolution, like Thomas Jefferson, George Washington and Patrick Henry! And there are ⁶ .... eighteenth-century gardens you can tour. For day trips, you can go to an adventure park, visit Jamestown—the first permanent English settlement in America—go fishing in the river, play golf and other sports, or watch the race cars in nearby Richmond. Williamsburg is easy to get to by car, bus or train. Check it out on the Internet!

2 Complete the chart with adjectives from the text. Then write more adjectives you remember.

places	*historic*
people	
weather	
tourist attractions	

3 Complete column A with ideas from the text in Exercise 1.

	A Williamsburg	B My favorite vacation destination: ....
Introduction: Where is it? What are the people like? When is the best time to visit and why?	*Eastern Virginia*	
What is there to see and do?		
Conclusion: How can you get there? Where can you get more information?		

4 Add ideas for your own favorite vacation destination to column B.

5 Write a travel guide in three paragraphs. Use your ideas and the adjectives and phrases from Exercises 2, 3 and 4.

....
....
....
....
....
....
....
....
....
....
....
....

Vocabulary • Household chores

★ **1** Match the verbs (1–8) to the nouns (a–h).

1 clear	a the floor
2 do	b the trash
3 feed	c the laundry
4 sweep	d the car
5 make	e the table
6 hang out	f the cat
7 take out	g the ironing
8 wash	h your bed

★★ **2** Complete the sentences with the correct form of these verbs.

cook	do	wash	set
load	mow	vacuum	~~walk~~

1 Who's going to *walk* the dog this afternoon?
2 It's raining! Did you .... the car this morning?
3 You .... the dishwasher, but you didn't turn it on!
4 Is it your turn to .... lunch?
5 You need to .... the lawn today!
6 Could you .... the table for six, please?
7 I .... the dishes yesterday!
8 Have you .... the carpet yet?

★★ **3** Choose the correct options.

1 Breakfast is finished! We need someone to *set / clear* the table!
2 Jonathan! Have you *made / done* your bed yet?
3 No brooms, please! It's much better to *sweep / vacuum* the floor.
4 The clothes are washed. You can *run / hang out* the laundry now!
5 Here's the clean laundry. Whose turn is it to *make / do* the ironing?
6 Mom! Don't leave without *setting / loading* the dishwasher!
7 Angela! I need you to *do / take out* the trash, please!

★★ **4** Use the information in the chart to write complete sentences.

George's chore list

1 *George has cleared the table.*
2 ....
3 ....
4 ....
5 ....
6 ....
7 ....
8 ....

Vocabulary page 109

Reading

★ **1** Match the names (1–3) to the number of people in their families (a–c).

1 Becca   a four
2 Malcolm   b seven
3 Richie   c two

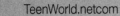

TeenWorld.netcom

← → C ⌂

Teens and Chores

On the subject of teenagers and household chores, we asked: What happens in your home? Here are some of the answers you sent us.

Becca

I don't have to do very much at home because we have a housecleaner who does most of the chores. But my mom says I must learn some things, so I make my own bed every day. She also says I must take care of my pets, so I feed the cat and walk the dog in the afternoon. But I don't have to do the dishes or anything because that's what dishwashers are for!

Malcolm

My sister and I have to help with the chores. My parents have a chart on the fridge door, and every week we switch activities. This week I must load and unload the dishwasher, and my sister has to set and clear the table. But she's five years younger than me, so I often have to do more than her. She never has to mow the lawn, for example, or do the ironing.

Richie

There are five children in our family, and our parents tell us we must do our share of the housework. The older children have to do things like cook meals and take out the trash. The younger ones have to do smaller chores, like clear the table and load the dishwasher.

★ **2** Choose the correct options.

1 *Becca / Malcolm* does a lot of chores.
2 *Malcolm / Richie* does more than his younger sister.
3 *Becca / Richie* has to take care of animals.
4 Only members of the family do the chores in *Becca's / Malcolm's* home.
5 The younger children usually do the easier chores in *Richie's / Becca's* home.

★★ **3** Complete the sentences.

1 Becca has to do *some* chores every day.
2 Becca doesn't have to do the ....
3 Malcolm can see his chores on the ....
4 Malcolm's sister doesn't have to do .... chores.
5 Richie gives .... examples of the chores for the children in his home.

Grammar • Have to/Don't have to

★ 1 Read the chart. Are the statements true (T) or false (F)?

	Millie	Mark
make the bed	✓	✓
do the ironing	✗	✓
do the laundry	✗	✗
cook a meal	✓	✓
walk the dog	✓	✗
mow the lawn	✗	✗
wash the car	✗	✓

1 Millie has to do more chores than Mark.   *F*
2 Millie and Mark have to make the bed.   ....
3 Only Millie has to do the ironing.   ....
4 Mark doesn't have to do the laundry.   ....
5 Millie doesn't have to cook a meal.   ....
6 Mark has to walk the dog.   ....
7 Millie and Mark don't have to mow the lawn.   ....

★★ 2 Complete the questions with the correct form of the verbs. Add the correct verb in the answers.

1 *Do you have to* (you/have to) clear the table? No, I *don't*.
2 .... (your brother/have to) sweep the floor? Yes, he ....
3 .... (your parents/have to) share the chores? Yes, they ....
4 .... (your sister/have to) take out the trash? No, she ....

★★ 3 Complete the conversation with the correct form of *have to/don't have to*.

A What kind of chores [1] *do you have to* (you) do at summer camp?
B I [2]...................... make my bed every morning.
A And outside your room? [3]...................... (you) work in the kitchen?
B No, I don't. The kitchen staff [4]...................... load and unload the dishwasher, and they also [5]...................... take the trash out.
A What about your clothes?
B We [6]...................... do the laundry because the supervisors do that, but we [7]...................... sweep the floor.

• Must/Mustn't

★ 4 Read the sentences. Write O for Obligation, N/O for No obligation or P for Prohibition.

1 You must do the dishes after breakfast!   *O*
2 We mustn't feed the cat more than once a day.   ....
3 I must make the bed before I go to school.   ....
4 We don't have to cook any meals on weekdays.   ....
5 My brother must walk the dog every morning.   ....
6 Joanna doesn't have to do the ironing every day.   ....
7 You mustn't wash the car in the street.   ....

★★ 5 Look at the rules for students sharing an apartment. Write sentences with *must/mustn't* and *have to/don't have to*.

Students' rules

① take out the trash before six o'clock   P
② do the laundry in the morning   O
③ hang out the laundry on the balcony   P
④ do the ironing in the kitchen   N/O
⑤ vacuum the floor at night   P
⑥ sweep the floor on the landing   O
⑦ feed the neighbor's cats   N/O

1 *We mustn't take out the trash before six o'clock.*
2 ....
3 ....
4 ....
5 ....
6 ....
7 ....

Grammar Reference pages 96–97

Vocabulary • Feelings adjectives

★ **1** Complete the definitions with these adjectives.

confident	confused	embarrassed
fed up	~~grateful~~	guilty

1 When someone has solved a problem for you, you feel *grateful*.
2 When you do something wrong and don't admit it, you feel ....
3 When you make a big mistake in front of other people, you feel ....
4 When you know for sure that you can do something well, you feel ....
5 When you don't know what to do and can't make a decision, you feel ....
6 When other people do nothing and you have to do everything, you feel ....

★ **2** Put the letters in the correct order to complete the text.

FEBRUARY 24

Tuesday

Another day of ups and downs! Evan appeared today with a new smart phone, which is much better than mine—I felt so [1] *jealous* (asleujo)! And I got my math test grade: 65. I was a little [2] .... (depositpinda) because I studied a lot and I expected a higher score. But Stella got an 80, which is awesome, so I felt really [3] .... (dalg) for her. She was very [4] .... (rovenus) the day before the exam because her parents promised her some concert tickets if she passed. So she's been happy and [5] .... (eladrex) all day! Then in the library this afternoon, I was feeling kind of [6] .... (yellon) because Toby wasn't there. Stella said he was in trouble because she saw him outside the principal's office, so I got worried. But then Toby appeared. It was only a message, so I felt [7] .... (liedreve) that there was nothing wrong.

★★ **3** Choose the correct options.

1 Our team has won the last three games, so they're *confused / confident* about winning tomorrow.
2 I'm *fed up / nervous* with waiting for the bus. I think I'll just walk instead!
3 Janet got very *guilty / upset* the other day when she lost her cell phone.
4 Reggie is a little *jealous / confused* because my bike has better brakes than his.
5 I fell down in class and everyone laughed! I felt really *disappointed / embarrassed*.
6 I lost my address book on the weekend, but Sadie found it, so I felt *relieved / relaxed*.

★★ **4** Complete the conversation with these words.

~~confused~~	embarrassed	fed up	grateful
lonely	relaxed	upset	

A Did you see the TV show last night? The one about the friends who share an apartment?
B Yes, but I got a little [1] *confused* because the story wasn't very clear. Who was the boy that got [2] .... because someone spilled coffee on his laptop?
A That was Adam. In general, he's [3] .... with his roommates because he's neat and organized, and they're not! Their way of doing things is much more [4] ....
B You mean careless! So who was the girl whose face went so red?
A That was Nikki. She was [5] .... because she got Thierry's name wrong, and the others laughed. And that's why she was so [6] .... to Lucas for helping her.
B OK, now I understand better. Do you watch it regularly?
A Whenever I'm feeling a little [7] .... , I watch another episode. It's great!
B Cool!

Vocabulary page 109

Chatroom Giving advice

Speaking and Listening

★ **1** Match the problems (1–6) to the advice (a–f).
24 Then listen and check.

1 I've been a little lonely recently. *d*
2 I'm tired of the same cereals!
3 I spend too much time on the Internet.
4 I miss my brother who's in Japan.
5 I don't get the presents I want.
6 I have to clean my room every week.

a I don't think you should complain. It only takes ten minutes!
b Maybe you should buy them yourself!
c Why don't you video call him?
d Maybe you should call your friends!
e Why don't you have toast, then?
f I think you should do more outdoor activities.

★ **2** Put the words in the correct order to make
25 answers. Then listen and check.

1 A I'm not sure this T-shirt fits me very well.
  B size / try / you / Why / different / a / don't / ?
    Why don't you try a different size?

2 A I'd like to learn how to draw well.
  B drawing / you / classes / take / Maybe / should

  ....

3 A I'm thinking about changing the color of my hair.
  B that / I / worry / don't / you / should / think / about / !

  ....

4 A I want to eat more healthily.
  B shouldn't / meals / Maybe / have / snacks / between / you / !

  ....

5 A I need a larger allowance.
  B chores / you / home / should / do / think / more / at / I / first / !

  ....

6 A There's no room in my closet for all my clothes!
  B new / I / should / many / think / clothes / don't / buy / so / you

  ....

★★ **3** Complete the conversation with these words.
26 Then listen and check.

~~fed up~~	I don't think	I feel tired
Why don't you	you don't have time	You should

A You look ¹ *fed up*! What's the matter?
B I have to get up very early for school, so ² .... all the time.
A Well, ³ .... you should go to bed so late!
B And I hate having to wear the school uniform. Why can't I wear my own clothes?
A ⁴ .... think about more important things?
B Like what?
A Like helping me with the chores! When you're busy working, ⁵ .... to worry about anything else.
B Yes, but I have to study. And I get good grades at school!
A So you have nothing to worry about. ⁶ .... learn to wake up with a smile!

★★ **4** Listen to the conversation in Exercise 3 again.
26 Complete the sentences with one word.

1 Speaker B always feels *tired*.
2 Speaker B doesn't like .... a uniform.
3 Speaker A's opinions are .... from Speaker B's opinions.
4 Speaker A says it's more important to .... things than to worry.
5 Speaker A says that B should .... to be more positive in the morning.

★★ **5** Write a conversation. Use expressions from Exercises 1–3, and this information:

A friend tells you about a problem. Give your friend advice. Mention two things you think he/she should do and two things you think he/she shouldn't do.

Speaking and Listening page 118

Grammar • Predictions with *will*, *won't*, *might*

★ 1 Choose the correct options.

1 I don't think our visitors *will* / *might* arrive on time.
2 They're not sure about the weather. They *will* / *might* stay home instead.
3 She's a big Justin Bieber fan! She *will* / *might* go to the Bieber concert!
4 He doesn't read. He *won't* / *might not* pass his literature exam.
5 We haven't decided. We *will* / *might* go to visit Elaine's family.
6 School is closed today. There *won't* / *might not* be anyone in the office.
7 Shane's a little confused. He *will* / *might* study to be a mechanic.

★ 2 Match the questions (1–6) to the answers (a–f).

1 Do you think our team will win?   e
2 Do you think she'll come to the party?
3 Do you think it will rain tomorrow?
4 Will John like his present?
5 Will Emma be glad to see me?
6 Will we get to the station in time?

a I know she will!
b With this traffic, I don't think we will.
c I don't know! He might not.
d She might, but she's working late today.
e I'm sure they will.
f I don't think it will. It's too sunny.

★★ 3 Complete the sentences with *will, won't* or *might*.

1 Uncle Tom's in China, so he *won't* be here tomorrow.
2 The hotel's next to a park, so it .... be very quiet.
3 The flight is on time, so Dad .... arrive in ten minutes.
4 I don't know what time they close, so they .... still be open.
5 The trains are very busy today, so you .... not get a ticket.
6 He's tired and nervous, so he .... be very happy if you make noise.

★★ 4 Make sentences.

1 our team / not win / because / not practice / hard enough.   (won't)
   Our team won't win because they haven't practiced hard enough.
2 Lennie / come / because / miss / bus.   (won't)
   ....
   ....
3 Jack / not want / talk / because / very upset. (might)
   ....
   ....
4 Grandpa / be disappointed / if you / not send him / a letter.   (will)
   ....
   ....
5 Chris / be embarrassed / if Sheena / tell / that story!   (might)
   ....
   ....
6 Tony / listen / you / because / too jealous. (won't)
   ....
   ....
7 Tina / not play / on Saturday / because / has a cold.   (might)
   ....
   ....

Grammar Reference pages 96–97

Reading

1 **Read the text quickly. Match the writers to their opinions.**

1 Caitlin   a pessimist
2 Brendan   b optimist

Homes of the Future

HOME   NEWS   COMMENTS   FEATURES   PHOTOS

Send us your comments on the article "Homes of the Future"!

Caitlin says

I feel confident that we'll have robots to do all the chores! I'm fed up with having to do the ironing and take out the trash. I've seen Japanese robots on TV, so I think we might have domestic robots soon. For example, my friend's mom just bought a machine that vacuums the floor by itself. If you don't have to do chores, there's more time to study—and have fun. I also think homes will be much greener, because the buildings will be better, and they'll use clean electricity from the sun, and things like that.

Brendan says

I don't think homes will be so different in the future. Some people might have robots, in the same way that some people now have housecleaners and landscapers to help around the house. But most people will still have to do their own chores. Robots will make you lazy. What will people do with all the extra time? Play more video games? There's nothing wrong with doing a few chores every day: we should all be able to cook and clean, for example. And I'm not sure about greener homes. Maybe some new homes, but not older ones, because people might not have the money to modernize them. In short, I don't think we should expect very big changes.

2 **Are the statements true (T) or false (F)?**

1 Caitlin doesn't like doing chores.   *T*
2 Brendan doesn't mind doing chores.   ....
3 Caitlin's friend has to vacuum her home.   ....
4 Brendan doesn't think there will be so many robots.   ....
5 Caitlin thinks people won't have to study so much.   ....

Listening

1 **Listen and complete the summary of the conversation.**

27

Max is worried because his ¹ *sister* is going to college. He says he'll ² .... her because there are no other ³ .... at home. The radio show host says that Max should be more ⁴ .... She says it's a good ⁵ .... to talk, but that Max shouldn't forget his ⁶ .... from ⁷ ....

2 **Match the expression beginnings (1–5) to the endings (a–e). Then listen again and check.**

27

1 give you   c
2 going away   ....
3 very lonely   ....
4 any other   ....
5 a great way   ....

a brothers or sisters
b to keep in touch
c some advice
d without her
e to college

Writing • A problem page

1 **Rewrite the sentences using *because* or *so*.**

1 I can't buy a cell phone because I don't have enough money. (so)
I don't have enough money, so I can't buy a cell phone.

2 They have a dishwasher, so she doesn't have to do the dishes by hand. (because)

....
....

3 You shouldn't get so upset because all friends argue sometimes! (so)

....
....

4 I can't mow the lawn because it's raining! (so)

....
....

5 Everyone went home, so I'm feeling a little lonely. (because)

....
....

6 I can't do so many chores because I have to study! (so)

....
....

2 **Read the problem and the advice. Answer the questions.**

1 How many reasons with *because* are there?
2 How many results with *so*?

3 **Complete column A with details from Ellen's reply.**

	A Ellen's reply	B Your reply
Paragraph 1 General advice	Recommendation:	
Paragraph 2 Specific ideas	1 show .... 2 explain .... 3 show .... 4 Mom talk	
Paragraph 3 Ending	Two things to remember: 5 .... 6	

4 **Read the following problem. In column B, write your ideas for a reply.**

All my friends have smart phones, so they can send each other messages all the time. I don't have one because my parents say I don't need one, and also because they say they're expensive. I would like them to change their mind! What should I do?
Alex

5 **Now write your reply to Alex in three paragraphs. Use your ideas and information from Exercises 3 and 4.**

Problem Page

Most of my friends at school have an account on a social network, so they're always in touch. They all know what everyone is doing—except me. I'm fed up because I can't talk to my friends or share photos with them! My mom says that it can be dangerous. But nothing has ever happened to my friends! What should I do?

Bethany

Ellen says:

Right, Bethany. Yes, that happens to a lot of teenagers, so we have some ideas to help you. But remember, you mustn't get upset because for many parents social networks are totally new!

The first thing you should do is sit down at the computer with your mom and show her the network because she might not feel very confident about it. And if she doesn't use a computer very often, she won't know how the system works, so you'll have to explain that as well. Maybe you know other members of the family—cousins, for example—who are also on the network. Show your mom their photos, their accounts and how long they've used the network. Then she should talk to your aunt or uncle so she can see she doesn't have to worry about you. Then she'll feel more relaxed.

Finally, don't forget your own responsibilities: keep your passwords secret, and don't accept people you don't know as friends.

Check Your Progress

Grammar

1 Complete the conversations with the Present perfect or Past simple form of these verbs.

come back	go	have to
hear	~~not see~~	stay

A Hi, Jan! ⁰ *I haven't seen* you for a while! How are you?

B Fine, thanks!

A You're looking very tanned! ¹ .... (you) to the beach?

B Yes! We ² .... (just) from the coast. It was great!

A How long did you stay?

B Ten days. What about you?

A I ³ .... at home since school ended. My parents ⁴ .... work this month, but we're going to Spain next week! Have you been there?

B No, but I ⁵ .... about it from friends who have been. It sounds like fun.

A I'll send you a postcard!

B OK!

know	meet	move	not talk	not write

A Who was that?

B That was my friend Ben. I ⁶ .... to him for ages! We used to be neighbors.

A How long ⁷ .... him?

B Since we lived on the east side of town. Why?

A His face looks familiar. I think I ⁸ .... him before.

B When was that?

A At Joanna's birthday party last month.

B Joanna? Tom said I should send her an email, but I ⁹ .... it yet.

A You should do it soon, then, because she ¹⁰ .... (just) to another school.

B I didn't know that! Tell me more …

/ 10 points

2 Choose the correct options.

0 Mom says I (don't have to) / mustn't have fish for dinner. I can have chicken.

1 The school rules say that we *don't have to / mustn't* use cell phones in class.

2 It's not necessary for you to wait any longer. You *don't have to / mustn't* wait.

3 You can't wear a T-shirt here. You *have to / mustn't* wear a shirt and tie.

4 If you drive in England, remember that you *must / don't have to* drive on the left!

5 Uniforms in this school aren't essential. You *don't have to / mustn't* wear a uniform.

6 Sorry, cameras aren't allowed in here! You *don't have to / mustn't* use a camera here.

7 He *will / might* be at home, but I'm not sure.

8 It's 2:30. Tom finishes work at three o'clock, so he *won't / might* be at home now.

9 Don't worry, Mom! I promise I *'ll / might* call you when I get to the station.

10 I don't know if there's another bus. I *won't / might* have to stay the night.

/ 10 points

Vocabulary

3 Choose the correct options.

0 When was the last time you .... camping?
  a got   **b** did   **c** went

1 Did you .... your tan at the beach?
  a book   **b** get   **c** go

2 Have you .... your bags yet?
  a packed   **b** checked into   **c** put up

3 Isn't it your turn to .... the laundry this week?
  a clear   **b** feed   **c** do

4 Oh no! I forgot to .... the dishwasher last night.
  a mow   **b** load   **c** sweep

5 Could you please .... the dog?
  a do   **b** vacuum   **c** walk

/ 5 points

4 Choose the correct options.

Did you hear the ⁰*report* / *blog* / *newspaper* on the radio this morning? They were talking about this 15-year-old girl who was walking down the street when two men ran out of a store in front of her. Two seconds later, a salesperson appeared, screaming ¹*happily* / *hard* / *loudly* for help. The girl was ²*lonely* / *confused* / *guilty* for a moment, but then ran after the men! She followed them down the street and around a corner, and saw them get into a car. She wrote down the license plate number ³*carefully* / *carelessly* / *sadly* and went back to the store. The salesperson called the police, and the men were arrested later that day. The store owner was so ⁴*disappointed* / *fed up* / *grateful* that he gave the girl a reward. You see? The interesting stories aren't just on the ⁵*international news* / *journalists* / *news anchors*!

/ 5 points

Speaking

5 Complete the conversations with these words or phrases.

an argument	I don't think you should
kidding	Maybe you should try
strange	Why don't you

A Jared and I had ⁰*an argument* last night.
B That's ¹....................... . You two have always been good friends.
A Yes, I know. But he wants to date me.
B You're ²....................... !
A No, seriously! And I'm not sure about what to do.
B Well, he's a really nice guy. ³....................... going out with him.
A Yes, but it might not work.
B ⁴....................... worry about that.
A But I don't want to lose a good friend!
B ⁵....................... think it over this weekend before you make a decision?
A That's a good idea!

| get there | How long does it take | Is it far |
| to buy souvenirs | We're looking for | |

A Excuse me! Can you help us?
B Sure! What would you like to know?
A ⁶....................... the Science Museum. How can we ⁷....................... ?
B Well, you can walk or take a bus.
A ⁸....................... ?
B It's about two kilometers.
A ⁹....................... to get there?
B For young people like you, if you walk, about 15 minutes!
A And is there a good place ¹⁰....................... there?
B Yes, the museum has its own gift shop.
A So, which way do we go?

/ 10 points

Translation

6 Translate the sentences.

1 I'm sorry, the 6:30 bus just left!

....

2 You're not allowed to put up tents in this area.

....

3 You don't have to come with us if you don't want to.

....

4 Would you mind doing the dishes tonight?

....

5 You won't find any mosquitoes here.

....

/ 5 points

Dictation

7 Listen and write.

28
1 ....
2 ....
3 ....
4 ....
5 ....

/ 5 points

(7) Make a Difference

Vocabulary • Protest and support

★ (1) **Match these words to the definitions (1–6).**

banner	~~charity~~
fundraising event	march
sign	volunteer

1 A non-commercial organization that helps people in difficulty. *charity*
2 A walk by a large group of people, usually to make a protest. ....
3 A large notice with a message on it, usually carried on a stick. ....
4 A person who offers to work without receiving money. ....
5 An activity that people organize in order to collect money. ....
6 A long piece of cloth or paper with a message on it. ....

★ (2) **Match the sentence beginnings (1–5) to the endings (a–e).**

1 Would you like to sign   e
2 We're taking up a collection
3 Would you like to make
4 Can you think of a good
5 Are you coming to the sit-in

a for the homeless people in our town.
b slogan for protecting animals?
c a donation to save tigers?
d at the local theater?
e our petition for safer schools?

★★ (3) **Choose the correct options.**

1 Andrea is a *banner /*(*volunteer*) for a children's charity.
2 That sign has a very clever *donation / slogan* on it!
3 Our school is having a *donation / fundraising event* this weekend.
4 We have a *collection / petition* with 50,000 signatures!
5 The *march / sit-in* starts at the station and finishes at town hall.
6 Don't miss the *demonstration / donation* in the park at nine o'clock!

★★ (4) **Complete the text with these words.**

donation	march	petition	signs	~~sit-in~~	slogans

Support our miners' [1] *sit-in* at the coal mine!

They've been underground for 23 days now!

You can help by

○ signing our [2] .... for better conditions
○ making a [3] .... to the support fund
○ taking part in Saturday's [4] .... from downtown to the mine
○ writing [5] .... for Saturday's banners
○ making [6] .... for Saturday (we provide boards and sticks!)

Vocabulary page 110

Reading

★ **1** **Read the text. Match the headings (A–D) to the paragraphs (1–4).**

A What can you do? B What do we do? C Why do we exist? D Who are we?

Integration Now

1 *D*

We're called Integration Now, and we're a local charity that works to help immigrants to adapt to local life. But we would also like local people to meet immigrants, ª *3* and share their cultures and traditions—without banners, without slogans. We believe that life together is going to be richer and more fun that way.

2 ....

We're here because when you move to another country, it can be very difficult to adapt. You will probably have language problems; you'll often have to ᵇ.... ; your children will go to schools with children from different communities. Even the food ᶜ.... ! So we'd like to help people integrate into their new community.

3 ....

We're a group of volunteers who work from a small office. We give information and advice to immigrants. We take part in local events so that local people can ᵈ.... . Our food festivals are especially popular! And we organize language exchange sessions: you can help people learn your language, and they will teach you some of theirs. Next year ᵉ.... to a bigger space for our own events.

4 ....

You don't have to give donations! Come and ᶠ.... with us. Meet some interesting people. You'll always learn something new!

★ **2** **Match the phrases (1–6) to the blanks (a–f) in the text.**

1 ask for help ....
2 meet immigrants ....
3 get to know them .ª.
4 spend some time ....
5 we're going to move ....
6 will be different ....

★★ **3** **Are the statements true (T) or false (F)?**

1 Integration Now works with both immigrants and local people. *T*
2 They organize a lot of marches and protests. ....
3 They mention four common problems for immigrants. ....
4 They work in a local school. ....
5 Not many people go to the food festivals. ....
6 It's not important to help by giving money. ....

Grammar • Be going to

★ **1 Match the questions (1–6) to the answers (a–f).**

1 Is John going to sign the petition?   c
2 Are you going to join the march?
3 Are your parents going to make signs?
4 What are you going to do with your old laptop?
5 Where's Ted going to study journalism?
6 When are you going to leave school?

a He wants to go to Washington, DC.
b I'll leave at the end of my fourth year.
c He says he is.
d Yes, I am. Definitely!
e I'll probably give it to my cousin.
f Yes. They're going to make six of them.

2 Put the words in the correct order.

1 **A** birthday / for / going / What / do / are / to / you / your / ?
   What are you going to do for your birthday?
   B I'll probably have a party.

2 **A** present / What's / to / Tamara / going / ?
   ....
   ....
   B I think it's a report on sports.

3 **A** teacher / going / exams / When's / the / to / math / grade / the / ?
   ....
   ....
   B She said she'll grade them next week.

4 **A** collection / Where / take up / are / they / to / the / going / ?
   ....
   ....
   B They'll probably do it on Main Street.

5 **A** write / are / slogan / for / going / we / to / What / a / ?
   ....
   ....
   B I'm not really sure. Let's think of something original!

6 **A** invite / Who / you / to / for / are / the / going / weekend / ?
   ....
   ....
   B A few of my good friends.

3 Make questions for the underlined answers.

1 We're going to organize a fundraising event.
   What are you going to organize?
2 It's going to be in the community center.
   ....
3 It's going to start at five o'clock on Saturday.
   ....
4 Johnny Depp's going to be there.
   ....
5 We're going to have a poster competition.
   ....

• *Will* or *be going to*

4 Choose the correct options.

1 I've read the menu, and *I'll* / *I'm going to* have the salad.
2 It's Candice's birthday soon. Maybe *we'll* / *we're going to* get her a present.
3 He's too tired to cook, so *he'll* / *he's going to* order takeout.
4 Susan said *she'll probably* / *she's probably going to* go shopping with me.
5 They bought the tickets. After the concert, their parents *will* / *are going to* pick them up.

5 Complete the conversation with the correct form of *will* or *going to*.

A Do you have any plans for next week?
B On Tuesday, my dad and I [1] *are going to* watch the football game on TV. And on Friday, we [2] .... probably go fishing, but that depends on the weather. What about you?
A The sales start on Monday, so my mom [3] .... buy me some new clothes. Then on Friday there's a concert.
B Who [4] .... play at the concert?
A A local band. One of my friends plays the drums.
B Cool! What else are you doing?
A I'm not sure. There's a circus in town this week, so maybe I [5] .... go to it. And you?
B I can't go out much. I have an exam on Thursday, so I [6] .... study for that.

Grammar Reference pages 98–99

Vocabulary • Verb + preposition

★ 1 Choose the correct options.

1 We're going to the demonstration because we don't *agree with* / *argue against* the new law.
2 I really *believe in* / *care about* the environment.
3 We haven't *decided on* / *worried about* a good slogan yet.
4 Ana is *hoping for* / *knows about* a good grade on her exam.
5 We think the factory should *apologize for* / *protest against* causing this pollution!

★ 2 Match the sentence beginnings (1–6) to the endings (a–f).

1 I can't agree   e
2 Mike should apologize
3 Anyone who cares
4 It's difficult to decide
5 I don't know anything
6 We're here to protest

a against the plans for another factory in our town.
b about the ice melting in the Arctic.
c for his silly comments.
d about sea life should join the march.
e with your ideas about teenagers.
f on the best place for a day trip.

Brain Trainer

Match these verbs and prepositions:

insist   about
believe   on
worry   in

Now do Exercise 3.

★★ 3 Complete the conversation with the correct form of these verbs.

> agree   believe   disapprove   insist   ~~protest~~   worry

A Hi! What are you ¹ *protesting* against?
B We don't ² .... with the council's plan to enforce a weekend curfew for teenagers.
A Really? I haven't heard about that.
B They're ³ .... on 10 p.m. as the latest possible time for teenagers to be out!
A Is that right? I don't think that's really necessary.
B Well, they say they ⁴ .... about all the noise for the neighbors. They say they ⁵ .... in everyone's right to relax on the weekend, and therefore teenagers should be home before 10 p.m.
A Do you have a petition I can sign?
B Sure! We have a petition for anyone who ⁶ .... of the curfew to sign.

★★ 4 Complete the text with the correct prepositions.

We're planning a march for next Saturday, and we're hoping ¹ *for* a crowd of at least 5,000 people to join us. The council wants to build a new landfill in the fields at the edge of town. But we don't believe ² .... landfills. We prefer to recycle all the garbage. And we worry ³ .... the plan, because that area is where many of us have picnics on the weekend. Our representatives have argued ⁴ .... them for weeks now, but they insist ⁵ .... going ahead with the project. So now is the time to show them how many of us disapprove ⁶ .... their idea. They must understand how much we care ⁷ .... our environment!

Vocabulary page 110

Chatroom Persuading

Speaking and Listening

★ 1 Match the comments (1–6) to the replies (a–f). Then listen and check.
29

1 Let's go to a demonstration! Come on, it'll be fun.   *c*
2 Why don't we join a march? I'm sure you'd enjoy it.
3 Are you coming to the sit-in with us? It's better than sitting at home.
4 How about taking up a collection for cancer research? Come on, it'll be fun.
5 Let's go to a fundraising event! I'm sure you'd enjoy it.
6 Why don't we make some signs? It's better than doing nothing.

a OK, I'll do it! They usually have food and music at those events, don't they?
b OK, I'll do it. Is that the sit-in at the theater?
c I don't know. I've never been to a demonstration before!
d I don't know. I'm not sure we have the right materials.
e OK, let's do it. What's everyone marching for?
f I don't know. The last time I did that, I only collected $10!

★ 2 Choose the correct options. Then listen and check.
30
1 Let's go on a march tomorrow! Come *on* / *off*, it'll be fun.
2 How about starting a petition? I'm *think* / *sure* people will sign it!
3 Let's invent slogans! It's better *than* / *that* doing nothing!
4 **A** Why don't we make a banner?
  B I don't *think* / *know*. It's very windy outside.
5 **A** How about starting a collection?
  B OK, *I'm going to* / *I'll* do it.
6 **A** Do you want to be a volunteer?
  B *I'm not sure.* / *I don't think.* It's kind of difficult.

★★ 3 Complete the conversation with these words. Then listen and check.
31

| I'll do that | it'll be fun | I don't know |
| I'm sure | it's better than | |

Alex	Why don't we go to the demonstration today?
Bea	¹ *I don't know*. It's pretty cold out today.
Alex	That doesn't matter! We can put warm clothes on.
Bea	True, but we don't have a banner.
Alex	² .... we can make one!
Bea	I don't know! I'm kind of tired.
Alex	Come on! It's for a good cause, and ³ ....
Bea	I guess ⁴ .... sitting on the sofa! OK, I'll do it. Let's get started on that banner.
Alex	⁵ .... , and you can make a sign.
Bea	OK, sounds great!

★★ 4 Listen to the conversation in Exercise 3 again. Are the statements true (T) or false (F)?
31

1 Everything is prepared for the demonstration.   *F*
2 Bea isn't sure about the idea.   ....
3 Alex says they can buy a banner.   ....
4 Alex persuades Bea to go to the demonstration.   ....
5 Alex will make the sign.   ....

★★ 5 Write a conversation. Use phrases from Exercises 1–3 and this information:

You're with a friend. You want to join a protest march, but your friend wants to play a video game instead. Persuade your friend to go to the march with you.

....
....
....
....
....
....
....
....

Speaking and Listening page 119

Grammar • First conditional

★ **1** Match the sentence beginnings (1–6) to the endings (a–f).

1 If you help me,   *e*
2 If you want to stay out late,
3 If you make the banner,
4 We'll clean up the kitchen
5 We'll go on the march
6 We'll plan the party

a if you think of some good slogans.
b if you send the invitations.
c if you cook lunch.
d I'll do the signs.
e I'll help you.
f you'll need to clean up your room first.

★ **2** The Romeo protests. Put the words in the correct order.

1 What will happen if / us / to / don't / they / listen / ?
What will happen if they don't listen to us?
2 What will happen if / the / stops / the / mayor / demonstration / ?
....
3 If she doesn't come out, / will / march / to / a / organize / we / have
....
4 If she doesn't come out, / slogan / better / a / have / invent / we / to / will
....
5 If she doesn't come out, / need / sign / more / we / to / petition / will / people / the
....

★★ **3** Write sentence endings. Use the correct form of the verbs.

1 If I do well on these exams, I / get into / the school of my choice.
If I do well on these exams, I'll get into the school of my choice.
2 If you access the webpage, you / get / a lot of good ideas.
....
3 If I don't get home on time, I / miss / my favorite series on TV.
....
4 Her mom will be worried if / she / not come / home on time.
....
5 His father won't be happy if / anything happen / to the car.
....
6 Your pet will get sick if / you / not feed / it properly.
....

★★ **4** Complete the replies with the correct form of the verbs.

1 **A** What are you worried about?
  B If I *don't find* (not find) the house keys, I'll be (be) in trouble!
2 **A** Will you wash the car?
  B If I .... (wash) the car, ... (you/give) me some money?
3 **A** Where are my glasses?
  B If you .... (look for) them, you .... (find) them!
4 **A** What's the capital of Mongolia?
  B .... (you/make) me some coffee if I .... (tell) you the answer?
5 **A** We're meeting at the café at 7:30.
  B .... (you/wait for) me if I .... (be) late?
6 **A** Sheena invited you to her party.
  B What .... (happen) if I .... (not go)?

Grammar Reference pages 98–99

Reading

1 Read the text quickly and choose the best headline.

a Teenager Gets a Job at a Magazine
b Teenage Protest Produces Results
c Teenagers Support Digital Photos

Who said teenagers don't care about the world around them? Who said that the only thing they worry about is chatting on social networks? Who said that protests never get anywhere? Here's a story to prove those people wrong!

In May 2012, a 13-year-old American girl went to the offices of a well-known teenage magazine to hand in a petition. She went there with her mother and a group of girls who agree with her ideas. What were they protesting against? They said that too many magazine photos show "fake" girls and women. They asked the magazine to be careful about how they use computer programs to change a woman's image. They said that girls need to see "something realistic" when they read their favorite magazines. Julia Bluhm, the 13-year-old, went into the magazine's offices and talked to one of the editors. As a result of that conversation, the magazine has promised to monitor how they process digital photos.

As you can see, protests can achieve results! If you feel strongly about a particular problem, you can talk to your friends and share your opinions. You can start a petition and collect signatures. People will probably listen to you if you present them with reasonable arguments. They might not make *all* the changes you would like, but *something* will happen! So, if you ask yourself "Can we change?," remember what a famous president once said: "Yes we can!"

2 Read the text again and choose the correct options.

1 People often say that teenagers *are* / *aren't* interested in current events.
2 Julia Bluhm produced a *petition* / *slogan* for women.
3 Julia and her friends protested against *all* / *some* digital photos.
4 They think that magazine photos of women *are* / *aren't* realistic enough.
5 The article concludes that change *is* / *isn't* possible.

Listening

1 Listen to the conversation.
32 Choose the correct options.

1 The *boy* / *girl* is interested in joining the march.
2 The *boy* / *girl* had a friend who went to the hospital.
3 The *boy* / *girl* doesn't worry about the weather.
4 The *boy* / *girl* worries about possible foot pain.
5 The boy decides to go on the march because of the *food* / *good weather*.

2 Who says these phrases?
32 Write B for boy or G for girl. Listen again and check.

1 I can borrow   G
2 we'll get wet   ....
3 these things happen   ....
4 I'll probably have to
  make a new one.   ....
5 Didn't I tell you   ....
6 All right, you win!   ....

Writing • A formal letter

1 Match the letter sections (1–3) to the examples (a–f).

1 Opening
2 Reason for writing
3 Closing

a Kind regards, *3*
b Dear Mr. Jones,
c I am writing to comment on …
d Best wishes,
e Dear *Teenmag*,
f I am writing because …

2 Complete the letter with these phrases.

> It is true   like my grandmother   So you see
> ~~The writer says~~   What can we do

3 Complete column A with information from John's letter.

	A John's letter	B My letter
Reason for writing	*doesn't agree with article*	
The problem		
A possible solution		

4 You recently read an article about pets that have been abandoned in the street. The article said that the animals should be captured and kept in cages at a special shelter. You don't agree with this idea. Write your main ideas in column B.

5 Write a formal letter to express your opinion. Use your ideas and the information and expressions from Exercises 1–4.

STAR LETTER

Dear *Teenmag*,

I am writing because I have just read an article in your magazine about older people living alone. ¹ *The writer says* that older people should all live together in special homes. I cannot agree with this idea. ² .... that some older people do not have any family to take care of them, but many of them do. My grandmother lives alone and is very proud of this.

³ .... to help older people who prefer to live in their own homes? Perhaps we could organize volunteer groups to visit them. If they have company, they will feel better. If we help them, they can teach us a lot too, ⁴ .... I learn many things from her that I don't learn at school!

⁵ ...., it shouldn't be necessary to take older people out of their homes if they prefer to stay there.

Best wishes,
John Noonan

....
....
....
....
....
....
....
....
....
....
....
....
....
....
....
....
....

8 Danger and Risk

Vocabulary • Extreme adjectives

★ **1** Complete the sentences with these words.

~~awful~~	burning	excellent
furious	huge	terrifying

1 The movie wasn't just bad—it was *awful*!
2 The bull we saw wasn't just big—it was
.... !
3 The other driver wasn't just angry—he was
.... !
4 Walking through the tunnel in total darkness
wasn't just scary—it was .... !
5 When we got off the plane in Miami, it wasn't
just hot—it was .... !
6 Have you read this? It isn't just good—
it's .... !

Brain Trainer

Arrange these adjectives in order of size:
big tiny huge small
Now do Exercise 2.

★ **2** Replace the **underlined** words with these adjectives.

exhausted	~~freezing~~	furious
huge	thrilled	tiny

1 I wasn't wearing enough warm clothes for
such a <u>very cold</u> wind.   *freezing*
2 We met Beyoncé in a store in New York,
and I was <u>really excited</u>.   ....
3 At the zoo, I saw a baby kangaroo, and it
was <u>very, very small</u>.   ....
4 After six hours of shopping, we felt
<u>extremely tired</u>.   ....
5 A truck crashed into a store and made a <u>really
big</u> hole in the wall.   ....
6 My parents were <u>really angry</u> when they
saw the phone bill.   ....

Vocabulary page 111

★★ **3** Put the letters in the correct order
to complete the text.

Last winter we did a mountain hike of about
20 kilometers. We walked for hours through
the [1] *freezing* (greenfiz) snow, until we reached
the top of this mountain. The views from the
top were [2] .... (netlleecx):
the people and cars in the distance were just
[3] .... (yint) figures. Then my uncle
took us to a special area, where we climbed up
into a [4] .... (eguh) tree. We had to
wait half an hour, but then we saw some wild
animals come to drink in the small lake. We were
[5] .... (helldirt) because they were so
close! And by the time we got back to the car,
we were all [6] .... (steedhaux).

★★ **4** Complete the conversation with these words.

awful	burning	excellent
freezing	~~huge~~	tiny

A Did you have a good vacation?
B Yeah, in the end!
A What happened?
B My dad found an apartment building on the
Internet that was really cheap. I mean, the
building was [1] *huge*: it had 15 floors! But when
we got there, we discovered that the apartment
itself was [2] .... for the five of us. It
had only two bedrooms and one bathroom!
A Oh no!
B And that's not all! The temperature outside
was about 40 degrees Celsius—absolutely
[3] .... But the air-conditioning
inside was really [4] .... I was so
cold I couldn't sleep!
A Was there anything good about the place?
B Well, the swimming pool was [5] .... :
it wasn't clean enough, and there were too
many people. But we were still lucky, because
the beach was wonderful, and the nightlife
was [6] .... ! So in the end we didn't
really spend much time in the apartment.

Reading

★ **1** **Read the article quickly and answer the question.**

Which person has experienced saving someone? ....

Last week we published an article on risks that people take. This week we asked you the question:

Would you risk your life to save another person or an animal?

Here are some of your replies!

Allie

I don't know! It's difficult to say, because I've never been in such an awful situation. I suppose if a child or a small animal was in trouble, I'd try to help. But I can't imagine that I would risk my life. I mean, I wouldn't jump into a freezing river, because I'm not very strong anyway. And I wouldn't run into a huge burning building either, because that's just too dangerous.

Ben

I'm a little impulsive, so I might do something without thinking too much about it. Last summer at the beach, for example, a little boy fell off a rock, and I was able to rescue him. I was exhausted afterward, but also thrilled. If anything happened to my family or my close friends, I'd probably try to help immediately. But I wouldn't react the same with animals—because I'm not an animal person!

Mannie

I don't think I'd risk my life, but in a terrifying situation, you never know how you'll react. I don't think I'd take any unnecessary risks, but certainly if I thought I could help, I would do so.

★ **2** **Choose the correct options.**

1 Allie *would* / *wouldn't* try to help a child or a small animal.
2 She *would* / *wouldn't* take any serious risks.
3 Ben *often* / *rarely* does things without thinking about them.
4 He *is* / *isn't* into animals.
5 Mannie *is* / *isn't* sure how he would react.

★★ **3** **Are the statements true (T) or false (F)?**

1 Allie has no experience of risking her life.   *T*
2 She's pretty sure she's strong enough.   ....
3 Ben knows that he would act fast.   ....
4 Ben would help both people and animals.   ....
5 Mannie would probably try to help if it wasn't too risky.   ....

Grammar • Second conditional

★ (1) **Match the questions (1–5) to the answers (a–e).**

1 If you had the chance, would you ski down a mountain? *c*

2 If there was an awful fire in the building, would you know what to do?

3 Would you jump into the water if your pet fell into a river?

4 What would you do if you had enough money?

5 Where would you go if you wanted an excellent adventure vacation?

a I don't think I would because I can't swim very well.

b No, I wouldn't. I'd just run for my life.

c I'd love to try, but I don't think I'm brave enough!

d I'd probably go on a safari in Africa.

e I think I'd buy a huge hotel for me, my family and my friends!

★ (2) **Match the sentence beginnings (1–5) to the endings (a–e).**

1 If someone gave me a bicycle, *b*

2 If I had to stay in the jungle,

3 If my family had an apartment at the beach,

4 We'd have a bigger dog

5 I'd learn to ride a horse

a I'd go there every weekend!

b I'd use it to go to school.

c I think I'd worry about the snakes.

d if it wasn't so expensive.

e if we had room in our apartment.

★★ (3) **Put the words in the correct order to make the questions.**

1 What would happen / if / father's / I / keys / my / car / hid / ?
What would happen if I hid my father's car keys?

2 What would I do / school / if / to / I / go / didn't / today / ?
....

3 If I didn't go to school, / get / would / trouble / I / into / ?
....

4 If I didn't live in my neighborhood, / live / where / would / I / ?
....

5 If I didn't live in my neighborhood, / miss / would / I / it / ?
....

6 What would I buy / if / a lot of / I / had / money / ?
....

★★ (4) **Write sentences. Use the Second conditional.**

1 If I weren't so tired, I / stay / watch the movie.
If I weren't so tired, I'd stay to watch the movie.

2 If this book were more interesting, I / finish / reading it.
....

3 If it weren't freezing outside, we / go / for a long walk.
....

4 I'd help you with your homework, if / I / have / more time.
....

5 We'd stay longer, if we / not have to / catch the last bus.
....

6 They'd be much happier, if / it / not rain / so much.
....

★★ (5) **Complete the answers with the correct form of the verbs.**

1 A Don't you know the answer?
   B If I *knew* (know) the answer, I *wouldn't ask* (not ask) you!

2 A Do you like the jacket?
   B Oh yes! If I .... (have) the money, I .... (buy) it!

3 A What's the matter?
   B If I .... (have) a map, I .... (not be) lost!

4 A Where did you hear that joke?
   B You .... (not believe) me if I .... (tell) you!

5 A Do you like my new shoes?
   B I .... (not wear) them, even if you .... (pay) me to!

6 A Should I tell him the truth?
   B He .... (be) very disappointed if you .... (lie) to him.

Grammar Reference pages 100–101

Vocabulary • Illness and injury

★ **1** **Read the clues and complete the puzzle.**

Across

4 This is the noise you make when you force air through your throat.

5 This injury makes it painful to walk.

7 You often get this on your skin if you have an allergy.

8 You might get this on your finger if you have an accident with a knife.

9 You can get this from fire or from the sun!

10 You have this when your body feels too hot.

11 This is a problem for the dentist.

Down

1 This usually happens after you eat too much.

2 When your head hurts.

3 This often happens after shouting too much at a football game.

6 My dad got this when he was moving heavy furniture.

★ **2** **Complete the doctor's sentences with these words.**

a cough	a backache	a fever
a rash	a sprained ankle	

1 I was walking down the street when I put my foot in a hole and fell down.
   You have *a sprained ankle*.

2 My dad was lifting a big suitcase, and now he has this pain.
   He has ....

3 I woke up during the night and couldn't stop making this noise.
   You had ....

4 My legs are covered with little red marks!
   You have ....

5 I'm too hot, I don't feel well, and I'm really thirsty.
   You have ....

★★ **3** **Match the problems (1–5) to the suggestions (a–e).**

1 a burn   *e*
2 a cut
3 a sore throat
4 a stomachache
5 a toothache

a Why don't you take some of this medicine?

b You should go to the dentist!

c Don't eat or drink anything until you feel better.

d You should cover that with a bandage.

e Put a lot of cold water on it.

★★ **4** **Put the letters in the correct order to complete the teacher's report.**

Most of the students this winter have had the usual [1] *coughs* (hugsoc) and [2] .... (dolcs). Three of them have come to class with a [3] .... (refve), so I had to send them home. Many of them also complained about [4] .... (shadecahe), probably because of the heating in the school. One boy showed up with a [5] .... (nurb) on his hand, obviously from playing with matches. But nobody has had any [6] .... (shears) this year.

What's the matter?

Vocabulary page 111

Chatroom Talking about health

Speaking and Listening

★ **1** **Choose the correct options.**
33 **Then listen and check.**

1 What's the *ache* / *matter?*
2 I have a sprained *nose* / *ankle.*
3 *Are* / *Do* you all right?
4 How *do* / *does* it feel?
5 Not too *good* / *better.*
6 How *do* / *does* you feel?
7 A little *better* / *worse*, thanks.

★ **2** **Put the sentences in the correct**
34 **order. Then listen and check.**

a What's the matter, Monica? ..1..
b It means you won't be able to walk for at least a week. ....
c You have a sprained ankle. ....
d Does this hurt? ....
e Oww! Yes, it does. ....
f What does that mean? ....
g Oh no! ....
h I was hiking in the woods when I tripped on a rock. ....

★★ **3** **Complete the conversation with these phrases.**
35 **Then listen and check.**

| a little better now | do you feel | does it feel |
| ~~I burned myself~~ | That's awful | the matter |

Jess	That looks painful! What happened to you?
Jack	¹*I burned myself* in the kitchen.
Jess	What were you doing?
Jack	I was helping to cook lunch. Fried fish.
Jess	So?
Jack	The fish slipped out of my fingers, and I got burning hot oil all over my hand.
Jess	²....................... ! What did you do?
Jack	My mom turned the faucet on, and I held my hand under the running water. Then we got a cloth with some ice in it, and came straight here to see the doctor.
Jess	How ³....................... ?
Jack	It's still a little painful. But what about you? What's ⁴....................... with your hand?
Jess	I was cutting up vegetables, and the knife slipped.
Jack	How ⁵....................... ?
Jess	Well, I was kind of scared because I don't like seeing blood. But I'm feeling ⁶....................... , thanks.
Jack	That's good. I hate seeing blood, too!

★★ **4** **Listen to the conversation in Exercise 3 again.**
35 **Mark (✓) the correct box.**

	Jack	Jess	Both
1 accident in the kitchen			✓
2 hot oil			
3 kitchen knife			
4 used cold water			
5 went to the doctor			

★★ **5** **Write a conversation. Use phrases from Exercises 1–3 and this information:**

You go to visit a friend, and you find him/her sick in bed. Talk about his/her health. Explain something similar which happened to you last year.

Speaking and Listening page 120

Grammar • Relative pronouns

★ **1** Match the sentence beginnings (1–6) to the endings (a–f).

1 That's the stadium   *e*
2 That's the singer
3 There's the store
4 This is the pump
5 She's the journalist
6 That's the wall

a who wrote the article.
b which I use for my bike.
c which I fell off.
d where I bought my bike.
e where our team won the championship.
f who gave me an autograph.

★ **2** Choose the correct options.

1 These are the photos *where /* which we took on vacation.
2 This is the guide *which / who* showed us around the city.
3 This is the restaurant *where / which* we had my birthday dinner.
4 These are the Chinese students *which / who* visited our school today.
5 This is the entrance to the theme park *where / which* I told you about.
6 Here's the river *where / which* we took a boat trip.

★ **3** Complete the conversation with *who, which* or *where.*

A Who are the people in this picture?
B They're the ones ¹ *who* went on the skiing trip.
A What happened to that boy on the left?
B He's the one ² .... got a sprained ankle on the first day!
A What a shame! And what's that in the girl's hand?
B That's the helmet ³ .... she wore to protect her head.
A And in the background?
B That's the park ⁴ .... we had a picnic lunch.
A What's that black thing there?
B That's the place ⁵ .... we made a small fire to keep warm!
A Nice! And are those your skis?
B No, they're the ones ⁶ .... I borrowed from another student. They were much better than mine!

★★ **4** Make sentences with *who, which* or *where.*

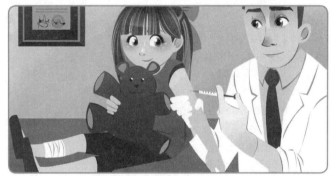

1 This is the dog / bite me / when / we be / on vacation.
 This is the dog which bit me when we were on vacation.
2 This is the park / everything happen.
 ....
3 Here's the car / my father / take me / to the hospital / in.
 ....
4 This is the doctor / look at / my leg.
 ....
5 That's the needle / he use / to give me a shot.
 ....
6 This is the nurse / put a bandage / on the bite.
 ....

Grammar Reference pages 100–101

Reading

1 Read the questions and choose the best answer.

2 Read the score box and check your answers.

Listening

1 Listen and answer the questions.
36

1 There are .... people in the conversation.
   a 2   (b) 3   c 4

2 They're talking .... .
   a in the hospital
   b at home
   c at the doctor's office

3 The boy had a .... accident.
   a walking
   b bicycle
   c car

4 He has problems with his .... .
   a knee and legs
   b eyes and neck
   c stomach and back

5 The doctor checked the injuries .... .
   a immediately
   b after an hour
   c after two hours

2 Who says these phrases? Write
36 **M for mother, S for son or U for uncle. Listen again and check.**

1 I'm much better   S
2 an awful accident   ....
3 sprained his knee   ....
4 How did it feel?   ....
5 Not too good!   ....
6 How did it happen?   ....

Would you know how to survive in an extreme environment?

Answer our questionnaire and find out!

1 If you got lost in the jungle, what would you do?
   a make a fire with a lot of smoke
   b find a river and follow it downstream
   c climb a big tree to check your location

2 If you were exhausted after walking in deep snow and it got dark, what would you do?
   a dig a hole in the snow and sleep inside it
   b lie down behind a big rock and sleep
   c try to stay awake and keep walking

3 If you were on a mountain and a terrifying storm began, what would you do?
   a get off the mountain as quickly as possible
   b keep walking until you found a cave
   c sit under a big tree until the storm passed

4 If you were walking in a meadow and met a huge bull, what would you do?
   a walk backward slowly and carefully
   b stand completely still and wait for the bull to go away
   c turn around and run away

5 If you sprained your ankle in the mountains, what would you do?
   a try to find an area with a signal for your cell phone
   b use a mirror to make SOS signals in the sun
   c make a fire with a lot of smoke

Score

a = 3 points   **b** = 2 points   **c** = 1 point

11–15 points: Congratulations! You know the right things to do!
6–10 points: You need to review your options.
1–5 points: You have a lot to learn!

Writing • An application form

1 Match the question words (1–6) to the answers (a–f).

1 Who   *f*
2 What
3 Where
4 When
5 Why
6 How many

a because that's our timetable!
b twenty-five
c school assembly
d in the auditorium
e at 8:30 in the morning
f my class

2 Make questions for the <u>underlined</u> words.

1 There are <u>five</u> people in my family.
How many people are there in your family?

2 We live <u>in an apartment near a park</u>.
....

3 <u>No</u>, I've <u>never</u> been abroad.
....

4 I'd like to go <u>because I think it would be interesting</u>.
....

5 I play soccer with <u>my friends</u>.
....

6 I'll be <u>15</u> next April.
....

3 Read the application form. Are the statements true (T) or false (F)?

1 Max can't run very fast.   *T*
2 He's had several pets.   ....
3 He probably likes taking risks. ....
4 He's not into rhinos.   ....
5 He probably wouldn't know what to do in an emergency in the park.   ....

4 Now complete the application form yourself.

LITTLE AFRICA SAFARI PARK ▌▌▌ ▌ ▌ ▌ ▌ ▌ ▌▌

Application form

Name: *Max Williams*   Age: *15*

1 How many of these things can you do? Mark the boxes.
swim ☑   run fast ☐   climb trees ☑
use a canoe ☐   take underwater photos ☐

2 How many of these things have you done? Mark the boxes. Say when you did them.
take care of a pet ☐
visit the zoo ☑   *I went last year on a school field trip.*
work with animals ☐
go abroad ☑   *I went to France in 2014.*

3 What kind of person do people say you are? Circle three words.
(quiet)   noisy   shy   (adventurous)   thoughtful   impulsive   patient   (impatient)

4 Which animals would you prefer NOT to see? Mark the boxes. Say why.
camels ☐   crocodiles ☐   hyenas ☑   lions ☐   rhinos ☐   snakes ☑
Hyenas are really ugly, and I'm afraid of snakes.

5 Write three things you would like to do in the safari park.
1 *ride a camel*
2 *see a crocodile*
3 *take photos*

6 Have you read the safety instructions in the visitors' guide? Yes ☐   No ☑

LITTLE AFRICA SAFARI PARK ▌▌▌ ▌ ▌ ▌ ▌ ▌ ▌▌

Application form

Name: ....   Age: ....

1 How many of these things can you do? Mark the boxes.
swim ☐   run fast ☐   climb trees ☐
use a canoe ☐   take underwater photos ☐

2 How many of these things have you done? Mark the boxes. Say when you did them.
take care of a pet ☐ ....
visit the zoo ☐ ....
work with animals ☐ ....
go abroad ☐ ....

3 What kind of person do people say you are? Circle three words.
quiet   noisy   shy   adventurous   thoughtful   impulsive   patient   impatient

4 Which animals would you prefer NOT to see? Mark the boxes. Say why.
camels ☐   crocodiles ☐   hyenas ☐   lions ☐   rhinos ☐   snakes ☐
....

5 Write three things you would like to do in the safari park.
1 ....
2 ....
3 ....

6 Have you read the safety instructions in the visitors' guide? Yes ☐   No ☐

Inventions

Vocabulary • Machine nouns and verbs

★ **1** **Match the sentence beginnings (1–6) to the endings (a–f).**

1 This product will run on a battery,   e
2 To turn on the machine,
3 Then use the keyboard
4 To attach files to an email,
5 If you want to watch TV,
6 Don't forget to turn off

a press the round button in the corner.
b click on the "Attach" button at the bottom.
c the machine when you've finished.
d you can also use the remote control.
e or you can plug the power cord into an outlet.
f to type in your password.

★★ **2** **Put the letters in the correct order to complete the sentences.**

1 Has anyone seen the *remote control* (meteor clorton)? I need it to change channels!
2 You can't play a car racing game without a .... (hewel) to move the car!
3 Oh no! The .... (trytabe) has died in the middle of the game!
4 It probably goes faster if you use the .... (beardyok) controls.
5 You have to plug in the power .... (rodc) first to turn the TV on.
6 If you press that .... (tontub), you'll delete all your work!
7 Take the cord out of the .... (teluto) before you go to bed!
8 This is a special plastic .... (beut) to keep all the electric cords in.

★ **3** **Complete the conversation with these words.**

button	cable	jack	plugged it in
press	~~remote control~~		turned it on

A What are you doing?
B We're trying to watch a movie, but we can't open the file.
A Have you selected the file with the ¹ *remote control*?
B Yes, that's it there.
A Have you checked the ² .... ?
B Which one?
A The one that goes from the computer to the TV.
B Yes, John ³ ....
A Yes, but is it in the right ⁴ .... ?
B I don't know!
A OK, I changed it. Now ⁵ .... the "Enter" ⁶ ....
B Hey! It's open! But I can't hear anything!
A You need to check the volume control then. Have you ⁷ .... ?
B Yes, that's it now. Thanks!

★★ **4** **Complete the text with the correct form of these verbs.**

attach	~~communicate~~	invent
plug in	press	turn off

How do you ¹ *communicate* with your friends? Sending emails was OK, until someone ² .... text messages on cell phones. Now cell phones do the same things as a computer, and they're much more convenient (unless you forget to ³ .... the battery to recharge!). Touch screens are amazing: you don't even have to ⁴ .... buttons anymore! I also use a special application that works with Wi-Fi. I can chat with my friends, and it's very cheap. But it can be expensive if you forget to ⁵ .... the Internet access or if you ⁶ .... a lot of photos or videos to a message.

Vocabulary page 112

Reading

★ **1** Read the text and put the paragraphs in the correct order.

1 C.... 2 .... 3 .... 4 .... 5 ....

A In the second stage, the drawings are computerized by the keyboard programmers. This is when the characters start to move. Then all the colors are attached, so the places and movements look real. These are like the building blocks for the whole game.

B The final stage is just as important as the other ones: game testing. A selection of players are asked to use the game and communicate any operating problems they find. Once these problems are solved, the game is ready for you to turn on and play!

C Most of us have shared an afternoon playing video games with friends, but how many of us know how the games are made? Let me tell you about the process in four basic stages.

D In the third stage, the parts of the story are put in order. Next, the player options are produced. This is done by specialized programmers. So now the game has its two key parts: the different levels of difficulty and all the tasks for the players.

E First of all, you should know that most games are produced by a team who work closely together. They have a lot of meetings where the basic story and characters are discussed. Once these components are agreed on, artists produce a set of drawings. The drawings illustrate the characters and the places in the game—for example, an old castle, a sports stadium or a futuristic city.

★ **2** Who does what? Match the actions (1–5) to the people (a–e).

1 invent the story and characters   *d*
2 make the first drawings
3 computerize the drawings
4 create the options for players
5 check the game for problems

a a group of players
b keyboard programmers
c specialized programmers
d the team
e artists

★★ **3** Are the statements true (T) or false (F)?

1 One person is responsible for the story.   *F*
2 The characters' movements are built in the second stage.   ....
3 Programmers do their jobs in the second and third stages.   ....
4 Most video games have three main parts.   ....
5 The testing stage is the most important one.   ....
6 Most games are developed in four different stages.   ....

Grammar • Present simple passive

★ **1** **Choose the correct options.**

Radio-controlled cars ¹ *is / are* operated by a remote control. Two sets of batteries ² *is / are* needed for the toy to function correctly. A large battery ³ *is / are* located in the body of the car, and a smaller battery ⁴ *is / are* placed in the remote control. A radio signal ⁵ *is / are* sent from the remote control to the car. The speed and direction of the car ⁶ *is / are* controlled by the buttons you press on the remote control.

★★ **2** **Match the sentence beginnings (1–6) to the endings (a–f).**

1 First, the cars are   e
2 Next, the design is
3 Then the parts are
4 Next, they are
5 Then everything is
6 Finally, the new cars are

a checked by computer.
b transported to the showrooms.
c produced in a factory.
d assembled in another factory.
e designed in the laboratory.
f created by the engineers.

★★ **3** **Complete the questions, then add the correct answers.**

1 *Are* cars made in Korea?
Yes, *they are.*
2 .... olive oil produced in England?
No, ...
3 .... cell phones repaired here?
No, ...
4 ....phone batteries sold separately?
Yes, sometimes ....
5 .... rice grown in China?
Yes, ...
6 .... batteries provided with all your products?
No, ...
7 .... these TVs equipped with the necessary cables?
Yes, some of them ....

★★ **4** **Make questions.**

1 **A** Where / the best cars / produce?
Where are the best cars produced?
B In Germany!
2 **A** these oranges / grow / locally?
....
B No, they aren't.
3 **A** How / this program / install / on the computer?
....
B By following the instructions on the screen!
4 **A** Why / the cables / not provide / with the TVs?
....
B Because different people use different cables!
5 **A** Where / those watches / sell?
....
B Only in specialized shops.
6 **A** How / these trucks / build?
....
B I really don't know!

• Active and passive

★ **(5)** **Rewrite the sentences in the passive. Include *by* + noun only if necessary.**

1 People in Italy design these clothes.
These clothes are designed in Italy.

2 Our chef prepares all our famous dishes.

....

....

....

3 Someone sells CDs like those in the street market.

....

....

....

....

4 We ask passengers not to stand near the doors.

....

....

....

....

5 The president of the club writes these articles.

....

....

....

....

6 People usually cook this kind of meat in a spicy sauce.

....

....

....

....

7 Shakira sings all the songs on this album.

....

....

....

....

Grammar Reference pages 102–103

Vocabulary • Word building

★ **(1)** **Choose the correct options.**

1 Cell phones have been a very popular *inventor /(invention.)*
2 Who was the *designer / design* of the first MP3 players?
3 We visited the capital, and we loved the old *builders / buildings* there.
4 Cars and video games are some of Japan's most famous *producers / products*.
5 Monet is one of my favorite *painters / paintings*.
6 I'd love to know more about where *writers / writing* came from.

★ **(2)** **Look at the text on page 77. Find nouns for the verbs (1–5).**

1 move   *movements*
2 select   ....
3 play   ....
4 program   ....
5 draw   ....

★★ **(3)** **Complete the words with the correct ending.**

1 I think the computer is the most important invent*ion* of all time.
2 For me, Goya is the most original paint....... of all time.
3 My mom doesn't like these modern build.......; she prefers old ones.
4 Our company sells only top-quality prod....... .
5 Armani is my sister's favorite fashion design........ .
6 What does this note say? I can't read the writ....... .

★★ **(4)** **Complete the conversations with the correct form of these words.**

build (x2)   ~~design~~   invent   produce (x2)   write (x2)

1 **A** Why are these shoes so expensive?
  B Because they're *designed* by Christian Louboutin!
2 **A** Who were the .... of the great cathedrals?
  B Nobody really knows their names!
3 **A** Why are these called personalized poems?
  B Because they're specially .... for individual people.
4 **A** What does a movie .... do?
  B He or she finds the money to make the movie.
5 **A** Who was the .... of TV?
  B A man named John Logie Baird.
6 **A** Are these houses strong?
  B I hope so! They're .... of concrete and brick.
7 **A** What kind of .... is this? I've never seen it before.
  B It looks like Chinese.
8 **A** What kind of .... are made here?
  B We make boots and shoes.

Vocabulary page 112

Chatroom Problems with machines

Speaking and Listening

★ **(1)** **Match the questions (1–5) to the answers (a–e).**
37 **Then listen and check.**

1 What's the problem?   *b*
2 Have you checked the battery?
3 Have you checked the earphones?
4 There might be something wrong with the connection.
5 Have you checked that it's plugged in?

a No, I haven't, and it's not. Yikes! I forgot!
b My MP3 player doesn't work.
c It's OK. I've checked it.
d They worked all right this morning.
e Yes, I bought a new one yesterday.

★ **(2)** **Choose the correct options. Then listen and check.**
38 **A** You don't look very happy!
What's the problem?
B The projector doesn't ¹*move /*(*work*.)
A Are you sure? I used it on the weekend.
B Well, it's turned ²*on / off*, but it's not showing the movie.
A There might be something ³*problem / wrong* with the cable.
B I don't think so. It's plugged properly into the ⁴*battery / jack*.
A Have you ⁵*broken / checked* the F5 button?
B Oh, right! That's it! You're a genius!

★ **(3)** **Complete the conversation with these phrases.**
39 **Then listen and check.**

~~broken~~	checked them
I haven't tried that	pressed the button
see the images	something wrong

A What's the problem?
B My digital camera is ¹*broken*.
A Are you sure? You were taking photos yesterday.
B I know, but not anymore.
A There might be ² .... with the battery.
B I've checked that, and it's OK.
A Have you ³ .... to turn it on?
B Yes! Look, the blue light's on.
A What about the settings? Have you ⁴ .... ?
B What settings?
A The symbols on the wheel.
B Ah no! ⁵ ....
A Well, try turning it around, to check the different symbols.
B Wait a minute. Now I can see the image on the screen!
A Let me look. Ah, you had the wrong setting. That's why you couldn't ⁶ ....

★★ **(4)** **Listen to the conversation in Exercise 3 again.**
39 **Write the three things they checked.**

1 ....
2 ....
3 ....

★★ **(5)** **Write a conversation. Use phrases from Exercises 1–3 and this information:**

A friend is having a problem with his/her video game console. Ask your friend to explain the problem; make suggestions about how to solve the problem.

....
....
....
....

Speaking and Listening page 121

Grammar • Past simple passive

★ **1** **Complete the questions and answers.**

1 *Was* the first smart phone produced in 1994?
Yes, *it was.*

2 .... more laptops than desktops
sold in 2008?
Yes, ...

3 .... digital cameras invented
in Japan?
No, ...

4 .... the first TV built in the US?
No, ...

5 .... your CDs replaced by MP3s?
Yes, ...

★ **2** **Complete the sentences with the correct form
of these verbs.**

catch	fly	forget	grow
keep	sell	sing	~~write~~

1 This famous book was *written* by Tolkien.
2 These songs were .... only
on special occasions.
3 Some scrolls were .... in libraries
for hundreds of years.
4 Kites were .... for the first time
in ancient China.
5 Thanks to the invention of books, old stories
were not ....
6 Fish were .... here until the river
became too polluted.
7 The palace was .... because
the family needed the money.
8 Cotton was .... in ancient Egypt.

Brain Trainer

**Notice what happens to the position of the main
noun when a sentence is transformed from active
to passive.**

Active: Tolkien wrote *this book.*
Passive: *This book* was written by Tolkien.

★★ **3** **Make questions.**

1 A cars / invent / in Germany?
Were cars invented in Germany?
B Probably, but I'm not sure.
2 A When / Lady Gaga's first album / release?
....
B That was in 2008!
3 A When / Michael Jackson's last concert / hold?
....
B I think that was in 1997.
4 A Which famous English musician / kill /
New York in 1980?
....
B It was John Lennon.
5 A What / Stephenie Meyer's first book / call?
....
B *Twilight.* It's her best-known book.

★★ **4** **Rewrite the sentences in the passive.
Include *by* + noun only if necessary.**

1 Americans reelected Barack Obama
president in 2012.
*Barack Obama was reelected president
in 2012.*
2 A tornado destroyed ten houses last week.
....
....
3 Police rescued three children from the ocean
on Monday.
....
....
4 Someone stole the school sports trophies
last night!
....
....
5 A teacher saw three cats on the school roof
this morning.
....
....
6 Ten thousand people signed the petition
to keep the local library open.
....
....

Grammar Reference pages 102–103

Reading

1 Read the texts quickly and match the names (1–3) to their preferences (a–c).

1 Natalia	a cars
2 Ted	b electric guitars
3 Chris	c Internet

>>>>>>>>>>>>>>>>>>>>>>>>>>>>>>>>>

Last week we asked you to tell us about your favorite inventions. Here is a selection of your replies.

Natalia

For me, the greatest invention ever is the car! Life wouldn't be the same without cars. Obviously, I don't drive yet, but I help my dad with our car. We watch Formula 1 races on TV, and sometimes we go to see the real thing if there's a race in our area. I get car magazines and read about the latest models. When I'm older, I'd really like to buy a red German sports car.

My favorite invention is the Internet! Laptops and smart phones are fun, but it's the Internet that makes everything possible. I can use it for entertainment, but also to study with. My parents do a lot of shopping on the Internet, too. But above all, I use it for social networking: I have to know where my friends are and what they're doing!

Ted

Chris

I'd say that electric guitars are my favorite invention. If we didn't have them, we wouldn't have any concerts, and life would be boring! Concerts are really important for me; they have such an atmosphere, and unlike CDs, you can really feel the music. But I also play the guitar and spend a lot of time practicing with friends. I learn a lot from watching the guitarists on TV, too.

2 Are the statements true (T) or false (F)?

1 Natalia only sees car races on TV.   F

2 Ted uses the Internet for three different reasons.   ....

3 Chris thinks studio music is the best.   ....

4 Natalia also plays a musical instrument.   ....

5 Ted's main priority is contact with his friends.   ....

6 Chris's main priority is music.   ....

Listening

1 Listen and complete the summary of the conversation. Use one word in each space.

40

Ally helps Ben, who has a problem with the [1] *video*. First they check the [2] .... cord, then the [3] .... cable and finally the [4] .... cable. Next, Ally suspects there might be something wrong with the input source on the [5] .... In the end, she uses the [6] .... to solve the problem.

2 Listen again and put these phrases in the order you hear them.

40

a in the wrong place   ....
b the hard drive   ....
c the power cord   ....
d Here you go.   ....
e It's both, actually.   .1.

Writing • An opinion essay

1 Put the parts of an opinion essay in the correct order.

a Second, using an e-book, you don't have to carry so many heavy schoolbooks. ....

b In my opinion, e-books are a really important invention. ....

c In conclusion, our life would be much simpler if we used more e-books. ....

d First, many different books can be stored in them. ....

e An important invention *1*..

f Finally, e-books save huge amounts of paper and trees. ....

2 Complete the opinion essay with these phrases.

> fast and safe   ~~important inventions~~
> my social life   that's not true
> the other traffic

<u>An invention I couldn't live without</u>

In my opinion, there are many ¹*important inventions*, but I couldn't live without my mountain bike.

First, it's my normal means of transportation. I use it to go to and from school every day. It's ² .... , it doesn't cost anything, and unlike ³ .... , it doesn't pollute the air. In fact, I have to be careful not to breathe all the fumes from the traffic!

Second, it's a great way to get exercise. Everyone talks about teenagers sitting on sofas playing video games and eating the wrong kind of food, but ⁴ .... for all of us!

Finally, it's an important part of ⁵ .... For example, on weekends I go out on trips with friends, and if I didn't have my bike, I wouldn't know so many people!

In conclusion, my life wouldn't be the same without my bike.

3 You are going to write an essay with the same title. Complete the table with your ideas.

An invention I couldn't live without	
Paragraph 1: introduction	1 ....
Paragraphs 2–4: reasons and example(s)	2 .... 3 .... 4 ....
Paragraph 5: conclusion	5 ....

4 Now write an opinion essay. Use your ideas, and information and expressions in Exercises 1–3.

....
....
....
....
....
....
....
....
....
....
....
....
....
....
....
....

Check Your Progress

Grammar

1 Choose the correct options.

0 Tell me your plan! What .... do you now?
  a will you   **b** are you   **c** are you going to

1 Her mom says that Sue .... leave until she's finished cleaning up her room.
  a won't   **b** doesn't   **c** isn't going to

2 I don't think I .... pizza—I'm tired of pizza!
  a 'll have   **b** won't have   **c** 'm going to have

3 They've already decided: they .... write to the newspaper.
  a 'll   **b** are going   **c** are

4 Here's the woman .... gave us the tickets for the concert!
  a where   **b** which   **c** who

5 These are the presents .... we bought for Dad.
  a where   **b** which   **c** who

/ 5 points

2 Make sentences.

0 She / take you shopping if you ask her nicely!
  She will take you shopping if you ask her nicely!

1 If you don't help me with the housework, I / not / give you a ride in the car.

  ....

  ....

2 If I / know / how to repair the camera, I'd do it for you!

  ....

  ....

3 If you don't leave some money for the waiter, he / not be / very happy!

  ....

  ....

4 What would happen if / not rain / all year?

  ....

  ....

5 If you had to go to school on Saturdays, what / you do / on Sundays?

  ....

  ....

/ 5 points

3 Complete the text with the passive forms of the verbs.

The world's first airplane took off in 1903 and began the race for better air machines. Many new kinds of planes [0] *were developed* (develop) between the two world wars. Jets and helicopters [1] .... (build) during World War II, and the first commercial jet flight [2] .... (achieve) in the 1950s. The Concorde, the world's fastest commercial plane, [3] .... (run) between 1969 and 2003. However, this kind of jet [4] .... (not produce) anymore. Today modern airplanes [5] .... (design) to use less fuel.

/ 5 points

Vocabulary

4 Complete the sentences with these words.

agree with	argue with	believe in
~~care about~~	signs	slogans

0 I signed the petition because I *care about* my community.

1 We spent all morning making the .... for the demonstration.

2 We wrote .... for our banners.

3 People join a march because they .... the reasons it was organized.

4 If we don't .... other people, there will never be any change.

5 I'm sorry, I don't .... your ideas!

/ 5 points

5 Choose the correct options.

0 **A** Why can't he walk very well?
  B He has a *stomachache / toothache / sprained ankle*

1 **A** Did you enjoy the movie?
  B Yes. It was *awful / excellent / burning hot*!

2 **A** What's wrong with your hand?
  B I have a *cough / cold / rash*.

3 **A** Isn't that pizza awfully big?
 B Big? It's positively *huge / freezing / thrilled*.
4 **A** I couldn't hear very well at the theater.
 B Why not?
 A The woman behind me had a *headache / burn / cough*.
5 **A** Have you read this story?
 B No, and I'm not going to. I've heard it's *furious / terrifying / exhausted*.

/ 5 points

6 **Choose the correct options.**

0 It won't work unless you turn this little .... here.
 a tube **ⓑ** wheel **c** keyboard
1 No wonder it doesn't work! It's not .... !
 a plugged in **b** produced **c** invented
2 Nowadays many people .... through chats and blogs.
 a attach **b** build **c** communicate
3 If you have problems with a power cord, try checking the .... .
 a batteries **b** outlet **c** buttons
4 What was the name of the artist who produced this .... ?
 a paint **b** painter **c** painting
5 Historians have discovered the name of the original .... of the monument.
 a design **b** designer **c** designation

/ 5 points

Speaking

7 **Complete the conversation with one word in each blank.**

A What's the problem?
B My cell phone doesn't ⁰ *work*. I can't make a call.
A Have you ¹ .... the battery?
B Yes, of course! Look!
A Have you tried ² .... the message button?
B No, I haven't.
A Well, this message ³ .... you don't have coverage! Anyway, what's the ⁴ .... with Ethan?
B He hasn't stopped working all week.

A ⁵ .... does he feel?
B He says he feels exhausted—and he has a ⁶ .... throat.
A Maybe he ⁷ .... lie down for a while. So, will we go out for dinner?
B I don't know. What about Ethan?
A He'll be fine! ⁸ .... on, it's only an hour or two.
B I shouldn't leave him alone.
A Why not? It's ⁹ .... than staying at home.
B I'll tell you what. We'll get takeout, and then we can eat here together.
A OK, you win! ¹⁰ .... do that.

/ 10 points

Translation

8 **Translate the sentences.**

1 If we don't protest, no one will change anything!
 ....
2 What kind of slogan are you going to write?
 ....
3 The first car was invented by Karl Benz.
 ....
4 What would you do if you had a stomachache?
 ....
5 If I were you, I'd check the battery in the laptop.
 ....

/ 5 points

Dictation

9 **Listen and write.**

41 1 ....
 2 ....
 3 ....
 4 ....
 5 ....

/ 5 points

Grammar Reference

• Present simple and continuous

Present simple	Present continuous
He works in a café.	He's serving coffee at the moment.

Use

Present simple

We use the Present simple to talk about:

* routines and habits.
  *We **get up** late on the weekend.*

* things that are true in general.
  *I **love** surprise parties!*
  *She **hates** news shows on TV.*

Time expressions

adverbs of frequency: *every day/week/year, on Fridays, on the weekend, in the morning, at night, after school*

Present continuous

We use the Present continuous to talk about:

* things that are happening at the moment of speaking.
  She's studying in France at the moment.

Time expressions

now, right now, just now, at the moment, today, these days

• Verb + -ing

Affirmative		
I/You/We/They He/She/It	like watching likes watching	cartoons.
Negative		
I/You/We/They He/She/It	don't like watching doesn't like watching	cartoons.
Questions		
Do I/you/we/they like watching **cartoons**?		
Does he/she/it like watching **cartoons**?		

Use

We use *like, love, enjoy, don't mind, can't stand, hate* and *prefer* + verb + *-ing* to talk about things we like or don't like doing.

Form

The verbs *like, love, enjoy, don't mind, can't stand, hate* and *prefer* are followed by a verb ending in *-ing*.
*I **don't mind watching** football on TV.*

Spelling rules

most verbs: add *-ing*   *play → playing*
verbs that end in *-e*: drop the *-e* and add *-ing* *come → coming*
verbs that end in one vowel + one consonant: double the consonant and add *-ing*   *sit → sitting*

Grammar practice • Present simple and continuous

1 **Match the sentence beginnings (1–5) to the endings (a–e).**

1 Bill drives a taxi,   c
2 My grandparents love sweet things,
3 Gerry travels a lot,
4 My daughter plays the cello,
5 Susan enjoys baseball,

a and today he's flying to Russia.
b and she's watching a game right now.
c and now he's waiting for a passenger.
d and she's playing in a concert right now.
e and today they're having ice cream for dessert.

2 **Complete the conversation with the Present simple or Present continuous form of the verbs.**

A Welcome to summer camp! There are six beds in this room!
B I (want) ¹ *want* one next to the window!
C And I (need) ² .... one near the door!
D Tina! What (you/do) ³ .... ?
B I (put) ⁴ .... my things on this bed and the one next to it.
D Why?
B Because Becky (talk) ⁵ .... to the counselor now, and I (save) ⁶ .... this bed for her.

D OK, but you (have) ⁷........................ an extra pillow on your bed, and I (not have) ⁸........................ any. Can you give it to me?

B Sure! Here you go!

3 Write sentences.

1 **A** What / do / Tuesdays?
   What do you do on Tuesdays?

   B I / usually / go / the library.
   ....

   A What / do / today?
   ....

   B Today / I / study / for an exam.
   ....

2 **A** Where / Amy / live?
   ....

   B Her family / have / house / on the coast.
   .... ,

   but she / live / here with her aunt / at the moment.
   ....

3 **A** What / John / do / right now?
   ....

   B He / wait / for the bus.
   ....

   A What time / it / leave?
   ....

   B I / be / not / sure. Maybe / it / be / late.
   ....

• Verb + -ing

4 Complete the text with the correct form of these verbs.

do	have	listen	live
~~look~~	take	wait	watch

We live in an apartment on the tenth floor! I like ¹ *looking* out of the window at all the people down in the street, and I love ²........................ to the rain on the walls when there's a storm. We can see the station too, and my grandfather enjoys ³........................ all the trains come and go. But there are some things I don't like very much. I don't mind ⁴........................ the dog out for a walk because I love the fresh air, but I hate ⁵........................ to take the trash out to the trash cans. I prefer ⁶........................ until

someone else goes down, then my brother or my parents take it out. And I can't stand ⁷........................ the dishes because I always spill some water on the floor, and I have to clean it up later. I love ⁸........................ so high up, because I don't feel so small anymore.

5 Put the words in the correct order.

1 doesn't / morning / mind / his / He / bed / in / making / the
   He doesn't mind making his bed in the morning.

2 coffee / mother / enjoys / on / My / the / having / patio
   ....

3 attic / Peter / alone / hates / in / being / the / !
   ....

4 front / like / sitting / bus / at / doesn't / the / of / She / the
   ....

5 loves / fireplace / watching / the / in / Katy / the / flames
   ....

6 stand / I / to / can't / smoking / next / people / me
   ....

7 across / The / running / dogs / yard / love / the
   ....

8 blinds / Pat / with / the / sleeping / closed / prefers
   ....

Grammar Reference

• Past simple

Regular verbs: affirmative and negative		
I/You/He/She/It/We/They	lived	in an old house.
I/You/He/She/It/We/They	didn't (did not) live	in an old house.

Irregular verbs: affirmative and negative		
I/You/He/She/It/We/They	went	to New York.
I/You/He/She/It/We/They	didn't (did not) go	to New York.

Regular verbs: questions and short answers
Did I/you/he/she/it/we/they graduate from college? Yes, I/you/he/she/it/we/they did. No, I/you/he/she/it/we/they didn't (did not).

Irregular verbs: questions and short answers
Did I/you/he/she/it/we/they see a ghost? Yes, I/you/he/she/it/we/they did. No, I/you/he/she/it/we/they didn't (did not).

Wh questions
What did he do?   Where did they go?

Use

We use the Past simple to talk about:

* finished actions in the past.
  *I **went** to the beach last weekend.*

Time expressions

adverbials of past time: *last night/week/month/year, an hour/week/year ago, in 2001, in the 20th century*

• Past continuous

Affirmative		
I/He/She/It You/We/They	was talking were talking	in class.

Negative		
I/He/She/It You/We/They	wasn't (was not) talking weren't (were not) talking	in class.

Questions and short answers	
Was I/he/she/it talking in class?	Yes, I/he/she/it was. No, I/he/she/it wasn't.
Were you/we/they talking in class?	Yes, you/we/they were. No, you/we/they weren't.

Wh questions
What were they doing in the library yesterday?

Use

We use the Past continuous to talk about:

* an action in progress in the past.
  *Sean and I **were talking** about you last night!*

Time expressions

often used with particular points in past time: *yesterday morning, at 7 o'clock last Sunday, in the summer of 2014*

• Past simple vs Past continuous

long action	short action
We were taking a photo	when a man walked in front of the camera.

short action	long action
A man walked in front of the camera	while we were taking a photo.

Use

We often use both tenses together in order to distinguish between different actions.

* Past continuous for a longer action in progress.
* Past simple for a shorter action interrupting the other.
* *while* introduces a longer action.
* *when* introduces a shorter action.

Grammar practice • Past simple

1 Make sentences with the Past simple.

1 My aunt / show / us / beautiful photos /
of her childhood.
*My aunt showed us beautiful photos
of her childhood.*

2 Our cousins / take / a lot of / silly pictures /
on / their school trip.
....

3 Their photos / be / blurry.
....

4 The album / be / full of / old-fashioned photos.
....

5 My friend / buy / a book / with dramatic
wildlife photos.
....

6 The local newspaper / print / colorful pictures /
of our school's sports teams.
....

7 The photos / of the fire / look / fake.
....

• Past continuous

2 Complete the sentences with the Past continuous form of these verbs.

| cry | have | look | play | ~~talk~~ | watch |

1 Mrs. Wilson *was talking* to her mother
on the phone.
2 Mrs. Jones's baby .... in bed.
3 The young couple downstairs ....
a boring conversation.
4 Mr. Smith .... an old-fashioned
movie on TV.
5 The family .... an interesting game
of cards.
6 Danny and Tom .... at photos.

3 Make questions with the Past continuous. Complete the answers with the correct verb.

1 Ian / clean / his room / this morning?
Was Ian cleaning his room this morning?
Yes, he *was.*

2 you / take / photography lessons / last month
....
....
No, I ....

3 neighbors / tell / funny stories / last weekend?
....
....
Yes, they ....

4 Shane / make coffee / just now?
....
No, he ....

5 the girls / read / colorful magazines?
....
No, they ....

• Past simple vs Past continuous

4 Complete the sentences with *when* or *while*.

1 Maria had coffee *while* Max was doing
the shopping.
2 We were walking home ....
we saw the fire.
3 .... the plane landed, Elena was
waiting at the airport.
4 .... Richard was checking
the map, I got some gas.

5 Complete the conversations with the correct form of the verbs.

1 A What [1] *were you doing* (you/do) when I
[2] .... (arrive) just now?
B Tammi [3] .... (play) the piano, and
we [4] .... (paint) in the kitchen.
A I thought the phone [5] .... (ring).
B I don't think so. We [6] .... (not
hear) anything.
2 A How [7] .... (your brother/take)
this blurry photo of a horse?
B He [8] .... (wait) for the right
moment, when someone [9] ....
(walk) into him.
A And then what [10] .... (happen)?
B While I [11] .... (help) him, the
horse [12] .... (run away)!

Grammar Reference

• Comparatives and superlatives

Short adjectives	Comparatives	Superlatives
tall	taller (than)	the tallest
big	bigger (than)	the biggest
large	larger (than)	the largest
happy	happier (than)	the happiest

Long adjectives	Comparatives	Superlatives
popular	more popular (than)	the most popular
interesting	more interesting (than)	the most interesting

Irregular adjectives	Comparatives	Superlatives
good	better (than)	the best
bad	worse (than)	the worst

Use

- We use comparative adjectives to compare two people or things.
  *My hair is **longer** than Angela's.*
- We use superlative adjectives to compare one person or thing to others in a group.
  *Angela has the **shortest** hair in the class.*

Form

Short adjectives	Comparatives	Superlatives
most adjectives:	add -er small → smaller	add the + -est small → the smallest
adjectives that end in one vowel + one consonant:	double the consonant and add -er big → bigger	double the consonant and add the + -est big → the biggest
adjectives that end in -e:	add -r nice → nicer	add the + -st nice → the nicest
adjectives that end in y:	drop the y and add -ier pretty → prettier	drop the y and add the + -iest pretty → the prettiest

Long adjectives	Comparatives	Superlatives
	add more boring → more boring	add the + most boring → the most boring

- After comparative adjectives, we often use *than*.
  *Football is **more exciting than** tennis.*
- Before superlative adjectives, we use *the*.
  *Jack is **the funniest** boy in the class.*

• *Too* and *enough*

The jeans are too expensive.
The jeans aren't cheap enough.
I don't have enough money for the jeans.

Use

- We use *too* and *enough* to express an opinion about quantity (*too* = more than necessary, *not ... enough* = less than necessary).
  *It's **too** cold in here! Can you please turn the heat on?*
  *I'm **not** warm **enough**. Can you lend me a sweater?*

Form

- *too* goes before an adjective:
  *It's **too** hot in here!*
- *enough* goes after an adjective:
  *It's not cool **enough**.*
- *enough*, *too much* and *too many* go before a noun: *enough* time, *too much* milk, *too many* cars

• Much, many, a lot of

How much money does she have?	How many T-shirts does she have?
She has a lot of money.	She has a lot of T-shirts.
She doesn't have much/a lot of money.	She doesn't have many/a lot of T-shirts.
She has too much money.	She has too many T-shirts.

Use

- We use these words to talk about large quantities of things.
  *There were **a lot of** people/**many** cars in the street.*

Form

- We use *much* for uncountable nouns, and usually only in questions or the negative:
  *How **much** money does he have?*
  *She doesn't have **much** time.* (= She doesn't have a lot of time.)

- We use *many* for countable nouns, in the affirmative, the negative and questions:
  *They have **many** pets in the house.*
  *They don't have **many** neighbors.*
  *How **many** friends does he have?*

Grammar practice • Comparatives and superlatives

1 **Put the words in the correct order.**

1 know / most / person / the / He's / I / interesting
   He's the most interesting person I know.
2 suitcase / than / This / I / is / thought / heavier
   ....
3 here / home / weather / than / The / at / better / is
   ....
4 class / She's / in / popular / the / girl / most / the
   ....
5 car / new / old / than / is / better / the / Our / one
   ....
6 world / cousin / person / My / the / is / in / funniest / the
   ....

2 **Make sentences with the comparative or superlative.**

1 be / Poland / big / Spain?
   Is Poland bigger than Spain?
2 be / German / difficult / English?
   ....
3 Erika / tell / funny jokes / Brian.
   ....
4 That ATM / far / this one!
   ....
5 That café / have / bad sandwiches / in town!
   ....
6 Japan / be / noisy / country / in the world.
   ....

• *Too* and *enough*

3 **Complete the conversation with *too* or *enough*.**

A What did you do on vacation?
B We went to the mountains.
A How was the weather?
B The first week it was [1] *too* hot to go out climbing, so we visited the town. The second week it was cool [2] .... to go out all day.
A How about the food?
B We ate out a lot. But one day we had trouble in the mountains because we didn't take [3] .... food. How about your vacation?
A We went to Paris.
B What was that like?
A Mom wanted to go to the opera, but it was [4] .... expensive. Dad wanted to walk up the Eiffel Tower, but he didn't have [5] .... energy! I wanted to visit the Louvre, but it was [6] .... big to see everything in one day. There wasn't [7] .... time.
B Yes, I know what you mean. Vacations are sometimes [8] .... tiring!

• Much, many, a lot of

4 **Complete the sentences with these words.**

a lot of	How many	How much
much	too many	~~too much~~

1 I can't buy that shirt. It costs *too much*.
2 .... apples would you like to buy?
3 She's always very helpful, so she has .... friends.
4 I didn't sleep .... last night.
5 .... did you spend on your laptop?
6 I have .... books for this shelf.

Grammar Reference

• Present perfect

Regular verbs: affirmative		
I/You/We/They He/She/It	've (have) cleaned 's (has) cleaned	the house.
Regular verbs: negative		
I/You/We/They He/She/It	haven't (have not) cleaned hasn't (has not) cleaned	the house.
Irregular verbs: affirmative		
I/You/We/They He/She/It	've (have) done 's (has) done	the work.
Irregular verbs: negative		
I/You/We/They He/She/It	haven't (have not) done hasn't (has not) done	the work.

Regular verbs				
Have Has	I/you/we/they he/she/it	ever	visited	Arizona?
Irregular verbs				
Have Has	I/you/we/they he/she/it	ever	seen	a snake?

Short answers
Yes, I/you/we/they have. / No, I/you/we/they haven't. Yes, he/she/it has. / No, he/she/it hasn't.

Use

We use the Present perfect to talk about:

- actions or events that happened at an unspecified time in the past, but are relevant to the present.
  *John **has visited** China. (but we don't know when)*

- with *ever*, we ask questions about personal experiences.
  ***Have** you **ever listened** to a podcast?*

- with *never*, we talk about experiences we have not had.
  *No, I **haven't**. I**'ve never listened** to a podcast— but I**'ve visited** news websites!*

• Present perfect vs Past simple

Present perfect	Past simple
A helicopter has landed in the jungle.	A plane crashed in the mountains *last Saturday*.
Have you ever seen a helicopter?	Did it crash because of the weather?
I've never flown in a helicopter.	Rescue teams located the plane on *Sunday morning*.

Use

We use the Past simple to talk about:

- actions or events that happened at a specific time in the past.

Time expressions

Present perfect: *ever, never, before, recently, in my life*
Past simple: *last night/week/year, five hours/days/ months ago, in 2012*

Grammar practice • Present perfect

1 **Rewrite the sentences. Put the words in parentheses in the correct place.**

1 Have you been to North America?   (ever)
   Have you ever been to North America?

2 Which African countries he visited?   (has)
   ....
   ....

3 Has your brother anything for the school blog?   (written)
   ....
   ....

4 We've watched a current affairs show.   (never)
   ....
   ....

5 They answered all of today's emails.   (have)
   ....
   ....

6 I'm sorry, but I finished my report.   (haven't)
   ....
   ....

2 Write questions for the <u>underlined</u> answers.

1 He's made <u>the sandwiches already</u>.
What has he made?

2 They've been to <u>China</u>.

....

3 I've never won <u>a prize in the lottery</u>!

....

4 My aunt has two girls; she's never had
<u>a baby boy</u>!

....

5 Patricia's not here; she's gone to <u>Italy</u>.

....

6 He's interviewed <u>Lady Gaga</u> three times.

....

7 We've finally finished reading <u>the news</u>.

....

8 They've written <u>another excellent report</u>.

....

• Present perfect vs Past simple

3 Match the questions (1–5) to the answers (a–e).

1 Have you ever written a blog?   *a*
2 Have you ever been on TV?
3 Have you ever recorded a podcast?
4 Have you ever bought a newspaper?
5 Have you ever watched the local news?

a Yes, I wrote a travel blog for my class trip
   in March.
b Yes, I have. We recorded it in science class.
c No, I haven't. I read the news on a website.
d Yes. I've watched it on TV and on my laptop.
e No, but my friend was on a talent show last year.

4 Choose the correct options.

1 Kathy *has written /*(wrote) a letter to
   the newspaper last weekend.
2 That's my mom's new car. She *bought /*
   has bought it last week.
3 Where's Isabel? I *haven't seen / didn't see*
   her recently.
4 My parents *have gone / went* home
   half an hour ago.
5 Alex says he *never had / has never had* a pet.
6 What time *did you get up / have you gotten
   up* this morning?

5 Write sentences.

1 I / go to / beach / but / I / never go to / mountains.
*I've been to the beach, but I've never been
to the mountains.*

2 In 2013 we / visit Scotland / and / write /
travel blog.

....

....

3 We / download / podcast / but / not be /
very interesting.

....

4 In science class / we / write / three reports /
this week.

....

5 Amy / interview / two local journalists /
for the school magazine.

....

....

6 Complete the conversation with the correct form
of these verbs.

can not	catch	find	never hear
print	~~read~~	turn on	think

A ¹*Have you read* this report in the paper?
B I don't know! What's it about?
A A man was out fishing in the ocean one day
   when he ²....................... a fish.
B And?
A On the way home, he ³.......................
   he heard some strange music in the car.
B Was the car radio not on?
A No! That's why he ⁴....................... understand
   where the music was coming from.
B So what happened?
A When he cut the fish open, he ⁵.......................
   an MP3 player in its stomach!
B That's impossible! I ⁶....................... such a silly
   story! ⁷....................... the fish.......................
   the MP3 player?!
A This paper ⁸....................... some very strange
   reports recently.

Grammar Reference

• Present perfect + *for* and *since*; *How long?*

> How long **have we been** here?
> **We've been here** for five days/a week/a month.

> I **haven't read a book** since Saturday.

> **She's lived** in France since 2010.

Use

We use the Present perfect with *for* to indicate a period of time:
*We've been on vacation **for** two weeks.*

We use the Present perfect with *since* to indicate a point in time:
*We've been on vacation **since** Monday the 14th.*

We use *How long?* to ask about the duration of an action:
How long have you been on vacation?
How long have you lived here?

• Past simple with *just*

> You **just had ice cream.**

> You **just missed the train.**

> The menu **just changed.**

Use

We use the Past simple with *just* to indicate an action that happened a short time ago:
*The six o'clock train **just left**. (It's 6:03 now.)*
*I **just went** to the bank. (Here's the money I got.)*

Grammar practice • Present perfect + *for* and *since*; *How long?*

1 **Choose the correct options.**

1 We've lived here (for) / since six years.
2 I haven't heard that song *for* / *since* we were in Hawaii!
3 I haven't visited Germany *for* / *since* I was a child.
4 Our families have gone camping together *for* / *since* we were young.
5 It's been much warmer *for* / *since* the rain stopped.
6 She's only had that toy *for* / *since* three weeks.

2 **Make sentences with the Present perfect and *for* or *since*.**

1 Jared / not write / to his parents / March.
   Jared hasn't written to his parents since March.
2 You / watch / that show / hours!
   ....
3 Maria / live here / two years.
   ....
4 The weather / be / very hot / the 15th.
   ....
5 We / not stay / in a hotel / October.
   ....
6 Pablo / have to / stay in bed / five days.
   ....
7 I / not put up / a tent / last summer.
   ....

3 Choose the correct options.

1 How (long) / many have you had your laptop?
2 How long / many days have you had a cold?
3 How long / many has Jane been in France?
4 How long / many times have you visited the museum?
5 How long / many have we had to wait?
6 How long / many letters have you sent?

4 Make questions for the underlined answers.

1 My mom has made four cakes for the party.
   How many cakes has your mom made for the party?

2 He's had to walk to school since the beginning of the month.

   ....

3 I've worked here for six weeks.

   ....

4 We've been abroad three times.

   ....

5 Your dad's been at the airport for three hours!

   ....

6 We've had our new car since last April.

   ....

• Past simple with *just*

5 Match the questions (1–6) to the answers (a–f).

1 Where are the postcards?   c
2 Is Kathy at home?
3 Am I in time for the movie?
4 Is dinner ready?
5 Do you have my keys?
6 Are you ready to go?

a I just put them back on the shelf.
b Yes! It just started.
c I just mailed them.
d Yes! We just packed our bags.
e No. She just left.
f Your dad just put it on the table!

6 Put the words in the correct order.

1 He's feeling happy because / good / he / news / got / just / some
   He's feeling happy because he just got some good news.

2 She's feeling great because / test / passed / just / she / her

   ....
   ....

3 Mom's still a little sleepy because / woke / just / she / up

   ....
   ....

4 My sister's really excited because / planned / she / a / just / vacation

   ....
   ....

5 Tim's tired because / kilometers / walked / he / just / ten

   ....
   ....

6 I feel really good because / went / I / just / to / the / gym

   ....
   ....

7 Andy's laughing because / good / heard / he / just / a / joke

   ....
   ....

Grammar Reference

• Have to/Don't have to

Affirmative
I/You/We/They have to set the table.
He/She/It has to set the table.

Negative
I/You/We/They don't have to set the table.
He/She/It doesn't have to set the table.

Questions and short answers
Do you have to do any chores?
Yes, I do./No, I don't.
Does he have to do any chores?
Yes, he does./No, he doesn't.

Use

- We use *have to* when there is an obligation to do something.
  *I'm sorry, but we **have to leave** now.*

- We use *don't have to* when there is no obligation.
  *You **don't have to come** if you don't want to.*

• Must/Mustn't

Affirmative and negative		
I/You/He/She/It We/They	must listen	to her.
I/You/He/She/It We/They	mustn't (must not) listen	to her.

Use

- We use *must* when there is an obligation to do something.
  *You **must take** your medicine now!*
  *In the US, you **must drive** on the right.*

- We use *mustn't* to express prohibition— an obligation NOT to do something.
  *You **mustn't wear** shoes inside the house.*
  *You **mustn't take** photographs inside the museum.*

• Predictions with *will, won't, might*

Definite
I think she'll be relieved.
You won't have any problems, I'm sure.
Will they finish it?

Possible
I might see them tomorrow. I'm not sure.
He might not like the movie.

Use

- We use *will/won't* to express what we think of as a definite future.
  *I'm sure they'**ll be** very happy.*
  *We'**ll** never **forget** you!*
  *There **won't be** much traffic in the morning.*

- We use *might* to express what we think of as only possible, but not definite.
  *If you're here tomorrow, I **might see** you in the library.*
  *We **might not go** out if the weather's bad.*

Grammar practice • Have to/Don't have to, must/mustn't

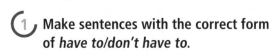

1 **Make sentences with the correct form of *have to/don't have to*.**

1 Sue can't go out because she / have / study.
   Sue can't go out because she has to study.

2 What chores do I / have to / do next weekend?

   ....

3 Did you / have to / work late / last night?

   ....

4 They're staying in a hotel, so they / not have to / cook / meals.

   ....

5 Do / we / have to / wear / suits for the wedding tomorrow?

   ....

6 Phil got up early, so I / not have to / wake him up.

   ....

2 Complete the conversation with the correct form of *have to*.

A What's it like at your summer camp?

B Some things are the same as at home. We ¹ *have to* get up early, and we
² .... make the bed. But we
³ .... do all the activities, because we can usually choose.

A That sounds OK! What about meals?
⁴ .... (you) cook?

B No, we don't. There's a specific activity in the morning if you want to learn.

A And at night, what time ⁵ .... (you) go to bed?

B Officially, we ⁶ .... turn off the lights at midnight, but most of us sit and chat in the dark until much later.

3 Life in the army. Look at the table. Write sentences with *mustn't, have to/don't have to*. (O = Obligation, N/O = No obligation, P = Prohibition)

1	get up late	P
2	sweep the floors	O
3	wash uniforms	N/O
4	iron uniforms	O
5	cook meals	P
6	get exercise	O
7	speak English	N/O

1 They *mustn't get up late.*
2 They ....
3 They ....
4 They ....
5 They ....
6 They ....
7 They ....

• Predictions with *will, won't, might*

4 Complete the sentences with *will, won't* or *might*.

1 Tom is sick, so he *won't* be in class today.
2 The weather is very changeable, so you
.... need an umbrella.
3 .... you bring me a souvenir from Sweden?
4 Jessie's in the backyard, so she .... (not) hear you.
5 It has snowed a lot, so it .... take longer to get home today.

5 Write sentences with *will, won't* or *might*.

1 I / not think / Shira / go / to the theater.　(will)
I don't think Shira will go to the theater.
2 Tamara / be / very upset, / so / she not go out tonight.　(won't)
....
....
3 Rob / invite you / to the party / if / you ask him nicely!　(might)
....
....
4 Where / you be / at five o'clock / tomorrow afternoon?　(will)
....
....
5 Diana / be / very smart, / but / she not know / the answer!　(might)
....
....
6 Reggie / look / tired, / but / he not give up!　(won't)
....
....

Grammar Reference

• Be going to

Affirmative

There are going to be 200 elephant sculptures.
The charity is going to make "elephant corridors."

Negative

There aren't going to be 200 elephant sculptures.
The charity isn't going to make "elephant corridors."

Questions and short answers

Are they going to make them?
Yes, they are./No, they aren't.
What are they going to do?

Use

We use *be going to* in order to express some kind of future intention or plan:
We're going to take skiing lessons this winter.
I'm not going to practice the piano today because I don't have time.

• Will or be going to

Predictions

In 30 years there won't be any Asian elephants.
You'll probably meet one in town this weekend.

Plans or intentions

We're going to save the Asian elephant.

Use

We use *will* to express a prediction:
You'll find the spoons in the drawer next to the stove.
Carmen will probably study chemistry.

We often use *will* after these expressions:
I think/I don't think, I'm sure/I'm not sure, maybe, perhaps.

• First conditional

if + Present simple, will + infinitive

If we don't protest, they will close the library.

will ('ll) + infinitive > if + Present simple

They will close the library if we don't protest.

Use

We use the First conditional to talk about possible situations. We feel these situations have a real chance of happening if the condition comes true:
If you don't hurry up, we'll miss the bus.
If it rains today, we'll stay home.

Form

If + Present simple, *will* + infinitive:
If the weather is good, we'll go swimming.

will + infinitive > *if* + Present simple:
We'll go swimming if the weather is good.

Grammar practice • Be going to

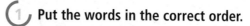

1 **Put the words in the correct order.**

1 A going / dinner / are / to / you / have / What / for / ?
   What are you going to have for dinner ?
   B Probably just some fruit and yogurt.

2 A put / Where / mirror / her / going / is / Jane / to / new / ?
   ....
   B I think it's for her bedroom.

3 A are / tattoo / you / to / Why / get / going / a / ?
   ....
   B Because tattoos are cool!

4 A theater / the / When / going / to / are / they / open / new / ?
   ....
   B Sometime in September, I think.

• Will or be going to

2 **Choose the correct options.**

1 David isn't sure about the bus. Perhaps *he's going to / (he'll)* take the train.
2 We like this place! *We're going to / We'll* stay three more days.
3 Ana has to work just now. Maybe *she's going to / she'll* join us later.
4 He just bought the tickets. *They're going to / They'll* travel on Monday.
5 They're flying to Mexico. I'm sure *they're going to / they'll* have a wonderful time.
6 I'm not feeling very well, so *I'm going to / I'll* take an aspirin.

3 **Complete the conversation with the correct form of *will* or *going to*.**

A What are your plans for the long weekend?
B We ¹*'re going to* have a special dinner with the family.
A What's on the menu?
B I'm sure Mom ².......................... cook turkey. It's her specialty. But later maybe we ³.......................... have a special dessert, because I'd like to try something different. What about you?
A We ⁴.......................... travel to Texas to surprise my brother.
B That'll be fun!
A Yes! He's been working very hard and hasn't been able to get home. He ⁵.......................... be really happy to see us.
B That ⁶.......................... be nice!

• First conditional

4 **Make sentences.**

1 If you don't practice enough, you / never / play well!
If you don't practice enough, you'll never play well!
2 If we buy one of these, we / get / another one free.
....
....

3 If you open this box, you / find / a surprise inside.
....
....
4 We'll catch the six o'clock bus if / we / be / lucky!
....
....
5 You'll probably find that information if / you / look / on the Internet.
....
....
6 I'll be very surprised if / Steve / not be / at home.
....
....

5 **Complete the replies with the correct form of the verbs.**

1 **A** What are you laughing about?
  B If I *tell* (tell) you, *will you keep* (you/keep) it a secret?
2 **A** I can't do my homework!
  B If I .... (help) you, ... (you/take) the dog for a walk?
3 **A** I don't like this food!
  B If you .... (not finish) your food, you .... (not get) any dessert!
4 **A** We're leaving tomorrow!
  B .... (you/call) me if I .... (give) you my phone number?
5 **A** This house is a mess!
  B .... (you/do) the ironing if I .... (vacuum) the floor?
6 **A** Romeo's gone!
  B What .... (Juliet/do) if he .... (not come) back?

Grammar Reference ⑧

• Second conditional

if + Past simple, would ('d) + infinitive
would ('d) + infinitive > if + Past simple
Affirmative
If I had an ordinary job, I'd be bored.
Negative
If I weren't a stuntwoman, I'd do extreme sports.
If I were scared, I wouldn't be a stuntwoman.
Questions and short answers
Would you be happier if you had an ordinary job?
Yes, I would./No, I wouldn't.

Use

We use the Second conditional to talk about unlikely/ unreal situations. We feel these situations have very little chance of happening because the condition itself is nearly impossible. The Past simple tense expresses this near impossibility.

*If I **had** the money, I'd **buy** a castle.*

*We'd **stay** longer if we **had** the time.*

Form

If + Past simple, would + infinitive.
*If I **studied** more, I'd **get** better grades.*

would + infinitive if + Past simple.
*I'd **get** better grades **if** I **studied** more.*

We use *were* instead of *was* for the verb *be*.

*If I **were** you, I'd buy a new phone.*
*If my house **were** bigger, I would invite all my family to come to dinner.*

• Relative pronouns

It's the place where I play soccer.
She's the woman who was in the car.
That's the cat which was under a car.

Use

We use relative pronouns to identify people/places/ things, or to give more information about them:

*That's the guide **who** showed us the city.*
*This is the hotel **where** we stayed.*
*These are the souvenirs **which** we bought for the family.*
*It's an object **which** we use to open doors. (= a key)*
*It's a place **where** you can relax and enjoy yourself. (= a vacation resort)*
*She's the kind of person **who** can tell you a lot of stories. (= grandma)*

Grammar practice • Second conditional

1 Put the words in the correct order.

What would happen if …

1 off / bus / school / at / didn't / the / get / I / ?
   I didn't get off the bus at school?

2 Saturdays / to / had / we / go / on / school / to / ?

   ....

3 with / man / the / spy / newspaper / were / the / a / ?

   ....

If I didn't take the bus, …

4 bike / school / by / to / go / could / I

   ....

5 time / get / on / wouldn't / school / to / I

   ....

6 rain / to / have / would / the / I / to / walk / in / school

   ....

2 Make sentences.

1 If I were you, I / not do that again.
  If I were you, I wouldn't do that again.

2 If this story were true, we / all be /
  in serious trouble!
  ....
  ....

3 If Dad saw you now, he / not believe his eyes!
  ....
  ....

4 They'd have to go to the hospital if his fever /
  not go down.
  ....
  ....

5 I'd ask for a refund if my flight / be canceled.
  ....
  ....

6 I wouldn't believe him if I / not know him!
  ....
  ....

3 Complete the replies with the correct form of the verbs.

1 **A** So you're going to be late?
  B Sorry! If there *were* (be) an earlier train,
  we*'d get* (get) there in time.

2 **A** Will Uncle Jack remember it's my birthday?
  B I .... (be) very surprised if he
  .... (not send) you a present.

3 **A** I don't know what to do!
  B If I .... (be) you, I ....
  (ask) your father for some ideas.

4 **A** You have too much luggage!
  B I know. If I .... (have) a car,
  it .... (not be) a problem.

5 **A** Can you see the animals over there?
  B It .... (be) much easier if there
  .... (not be) so many trees!

6 **A** Are you enjoying the walk?
  B It .... (not be) so difficult if the
  path .... (not be) so narrow.

• Relative pronouns

4 Complete the conversation with *who*, *which*, or *where*.

A Have you seen these photos before?
B No, I haven't.
A Well, this is the classmate [1] *who* had a fever,
  and had to go home.
B OK. And this?
A That's the science room [2] .... two
  students got burns in an experiment.
B How did that happen?
A They were using equipment [3] ....
  didn't work properly.
B Who's that girl there?
A She's the one [4] .... got a rash from
  touching frogs in biology class.
B Yes, that happened to a friend of mine, too.
  He played with some cats [5] ....
  lived near the beach, and his hands went
  all red.
A Is that the beach [6] .... we were
  on vacation this summer?
B No. It's a different one.

5 Make sentences with *who*, *which* or *where*.

1 This is a photo / the accident / I have / when I /
  be ten.
  *This is a photo of the accident which I had
  when I was ten.*

2 This is the park / it happen.
  ....

3 These are the skates / I be / wearing.
  ....

4 Here's the doctor / put the cast / on my arm.
  ....
  ....

5 This is the café / my father / buy /
  me an ice cream cone.
  ....
  ....

6 This is the nurse / write / a message on my cast.
  ....
  ....

Grammar Reference

• Present simple passive

Affirmative
It is made with plastic tubes. They are made with plastic.

Negative
The machine isn't made with plastic. Gloves aren't usually used to climb walls.

Questions and short answers
Is the machine made with plastic? Yes, it is./No, it isn't. Are the gloves used to climb walls? Yes, they are./No, they aren't.

Use

We use the passive when we want to focus more on an action than on the person or thing doing the action:

Coffee is produced in many different countries.

Form

subject + Present simple of *be* + past participle of the main verb

Coffee is produced in tropical countries.
Coffee is not produced in cold countries.
Is coffee produced in Africa? Yes, it is.

• Past simple passive

Affirmative	Negative
It was made by Ella.	It wasn't made by Ella.
They were bought yesterday.	The instructions weren't included in the box.
Questions and short answers	

Questions and short answers
Was it made from an aluminum can? Yes, it was./No, it wasn't. Were the instructions included? Yes, they were./No, they weren't.

Form

subject + Past simple of *be* + past participle of the main verb

The first cars were made in the late 1800s.
Cars were not built before the late 1800s.
Were the first cars made in Europe? Yes, they were.

• Active and passive

Active
Blind people use Braille. You write messages on a keyboard.

Passive
Braille is used by blind people. Messages are written on a keyboard.

Use

We use **active** forms when the person or thing doing the action is important:

Some people in Ireland speak Gaelic.

We use **passive** forms when we consider the action more important than the person or thing doing it:

Gaelic is spoken in Ireland. (= this is where we find Gaelic spoken)
Many buildings were destroyed in this city.
(= an important fact)

Sometimes we also want to specify the person or thing doing the action:

Gaelic is spoken by some people in Ireland.
(= not everyone speaks the language)
Many buildings were destroyed by fire.
(= fire and not water or other causes)

Most often, however, the person or thing doing the action is not mentioned:

Video games are produced in Japan.
Houses in this area are built of wood or brick.

Grammar practice • Present simple passive

1 Complete the sentences with the Present simple passive form of the verbs.

1 Our computers *are packed* (pack) in this department here.
2 The keyboard .... (attach) to the case.
3 The power cords .... (add) in a separate box.
4 The battery .... (produce) in a different factory.

5 The buttons .... (test) by that
   department there.
6 The remote control .... (sell)
   separately.

2 **Make questions with the Present simple passive.**

1 Where / power cords / plug in?
   Where are the power cords plugged in?
2 How / this tube / produce?
   ....
3 What kind of keyboard / use / in China?
   ....
4 How / the buttons / add?
   ....
5 When / the battery / attach?
   ....
6 Where / these engines / build?
   ....

• Past simple passive

3 **Make sentences with the Past simple passive.**

1 Horses / domesticate / over 6,000 years ago.
   Horses were domesticated over 6,000
   years ago.
2 Modern bicycles / not invent / until about 1885.
   ....
   ....
3 The first car factory / build / in Germany
   in 1885.
   ....
   ....
4 City bus services / begin / in England and
   France in the 1820s.
   ....
   ....
5 The first railway trains / run in England in
   the 1820s.
   ....
   ....
6 The first airplanes / not fly / until 1903.
   ....
   ....

4 **Complete the questions with the Past simple passive form of the verbs.**

1 When *was* the local theme park *opened*? (open)
2 Where .... the *Twilight* movies
   .... ? (make)
3 When .... the baby ....
   to its father in *Ice Age 1*? (return)
4 How .... Princess Fiona
   .... by Shrek?   (rescue)
5 When .... the ring ....
   into the volcano in *The Lord of the Rings*?
   (throw)
6 Where .... *High School Musical*
   .... ?   (film)

• Active and passive

5 **Change these active sentences into passive sentences. Include *by* + noun only if necessary.**

1 People make flour from wheat.
   Flour is made from wheat.
2 The school theater group performed this play.
   ....
   ....
3 Someone in Canada writes this blog.
   ....
   ....
4 The local factory produces one thousand cars
   a week.
   ....
   ....
5 Mark Zuckerberg created a huge social
   network.
   ....
   ....
6 A monkey stole our sandwiches!
   ....
   ....
7 Three boys discovered some old coins in a field.
   ....
   ....

Vocabulary ①

Home Sweet Home

Unit vocabulary

1 Translate the words.

Rooms and parts of the house
attic ....
balcony ....
basement ....
ceiling ....
driveway ....
fireplace ....
floor ....
garage ....
hallway ....
landing ....
office ....
patio ....
roof ....
stairs ....
wall ....
yard ....

2 Translate the words.

Furniture and household objects
alarm clock ....
armchair ....
blind ....
bookcase ....
closet ....
comforter ....
curtains ....
cushions ....
dresser ....
mirror ....
pillow ....
rug ....
vase ....

Vocabulary extension

3 Match the photos to these words. Use your dictionary if necessary. Write the words in English and in your language.

| chimney | elevator | faucets | ~~towel~~ | sink |

1 ....
....

2 ....
....

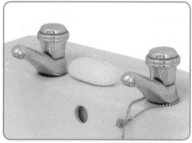

3 ....
....

4 .... *towel* ....
....

5 ....
....

Vocabulary

What's the Story?

Unit vocabulary

1 Translate the words.

Adjectives to describe pictures

beautiful ....

blurry ....

boring ....

colorful ....

dark ....

dramatic ....

fake ....

funny ....

horrible ....

interesting ....

old-fashioned ....

silly ....

2 Translate the words.

Adjective + preposition

afraid of ....

angry with ....

bad at ....

bored with ....

excited about ....

good at ....

interested in ....

popular with ....

proud of ....

sorry for ....

tired of ....

Vocabulary extension

3 Match the photos to these words. Use your dictionary if necessary. Write the words in English and in your language.

> annoyed about   ~~disappointed with~~   mysterious
> scary   surprised at

1 ....
....

2 ....
....

3 ......*disappointed with*......
....

4 ....
....

5 ....
....

Vocabulary

It's a Bargain!

Unit vocabulary

1 Translate the words.

Shopping nouns

ATM ....

bargain ....

bill ....

change ....

coin ....

customer ....

line ....

mall ....

market stand ....

price ....

products ....

sale ....

salesperson ....

shopping basket ....

vendor ....

2 Translate the words.

Money verbs

afford ....

borrow ....

buy ....

cost ....

earn ....

lend ....

pay by credit card ....

pay in cash ....

save ....

sell ....

spend ....

win ....

Vocabulary extension

3 Match the photos to these words. Use your dictionary if necessary. Write the words in English and in your language.

| bar code | discount | receipts | refund | ~~sell-by date~~ |

1 ....
....

2 ....
....

3 .... *sell-by date* ....
....

4 ....
....

5 ....
....

Vocabulary

In the News

Unit vocabulary

1 Translate the words.

News and media

blog ....

current affairs show

....

headline ....

international news ....

interview (n, v) ....

journalist ....

local news ....

national news ....

news anchor ....

news flash ....

newspaper ....

news website ....

podcast ....

report (n, v) ....

2 Translate the words.

Adverbs of manner

angrily ....

badly ....

carefully ....

carelessly ....

early ....

fast ....

happily ....

hard ....

late ....

loudly ....

patiently ....

quietly ....

sadly ....

slowly ....

well ....

Vocabulary extension

3 Match the photos and pictures to these words. Use your dictionary if necessary. Write the words in English and in your language.

cartoon strip   entertainment guide   front page
proudly   ~~quickly~~

1 ....
....

2 ....
....

3 ....
....

4 .... *quickly* ....
....

5 ....
....

Vocabulary 5

Enjoy Your Vacation!

Unit vocabulary

1 Translate the words.

Vacation

book a flight/hotel ....

buy souvenirs ....

check into a hotel ....

eat out ....

get a tan ....

get lost ....

go camping ....

go sightseeing ....

lose your luggage ....

pack your bag ....

put up a tent ....

stay in a hotel ....

take a trip ....

write a travel blog ....

2 Translate the words.

Meanings of *get*

arrive (*get to the campsite*)
....

become (*get cold*) ....

bring (*get the sunscreen*)
....

buy (*get a key ring*)
....

receive (*get a postcard*)
....

walk/move (*get on the bus*)
....

Vocabulary extension

3 Match the photos to these words. Use your dictionary if necessary. Write the words in English and in your language.

| book bed and breakfast | buy a travel pass | take a taxi |
| get sunburned | ~~stay at a youth hostel~~ | |

1 ...*stay at a youth hostel*....
....

2 ....
....

3 ....
....

4 ....
....

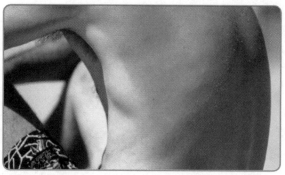

5 ....
....

Vocabulary 6

That's Life!

Unit vocabulary

1 Translate the words

Household chores

clear the table ....
cook a meal ....
do the dishes ....
do the ironing ....
do the laundry ....
feed the cat ....
hang out the laundry ....
load the dishwasher ....
make your bed ....
mow the lawn ....
set the table ....
sweep the floor ....
take out the trash ....
vacuum the floor ....
walk the dog ....
wash the car ....

2 Translate the words.

Feelings adjectives

confident ....
confused ....
disappointed ....
embarrassed ....
fed up ....
glad ....
grateful ....
guilty ....
jealous ....
lonely ....
nervous ....
relaxed ....
relieved ....
upset ....

Vocabulary extension

3 Match the photos to these words. Use your dictionary if necessary. Write the words in English and in your language.

~~anxious~~   carefree   change the sheets
mop the floor   water the plants

1 ....
....

2 ....
....

3 ....
....

4 ....*anxious*.............
....

5 ....
....

Vocabulary

Make a Difference

Unit vocabulary

1 Translate the words.

Protest and support
banner ....
charity ....
collection ....
demonstration ....
donation ....
fundraising event ....
march ....
petition ....
sign ....
sit-in ....
slogan ....
volunteer ....

2 Translate the words.

Verb + preposition
agree with ....
apologize for ....
argue with ....
believe in ....
care about ....
decide on ....
disapprove of ....
hope for ....
insist on ....
know about ....
protest against ....
worry about ....

Vocabulary extension

3 Match the photos to these words. Use your dictionary if necessary. Write the words in English and in your language.

| campaign for/against | disaster relief | ~~endangered species~~ |
| human rights | minority group | |

1 ....
....

2 ....
....

3 ....._endangered species_.....
....

4 ....
....

5 ....
....

Vocabulary 8

Danger and Risk

Unit vocabulary

1 Translate the words.

Extreme adjectives

awful ....

burning ....

excellent ....

exhausted ....

freezing ....

furious ....

huge ....

terrifying ....

thrilled ....

tiny ....

2 Translate the words.

Illness and injury

a backache ....

a burn ....

a cold ....

a cough ....

a cut ....

a fever ....

a headache ....

a rash ....

a sore throat ....

a sprained ankle ....

a stomachache ....

a toothache ....

Vocabulary extension

3 Match the photos to these words. Use your dictionary if necessary. Write the words in English and in your language.

| bandage delighted ~~horrified~~ needle cast |

1 ....
....

2 ....*horrified*.............
....

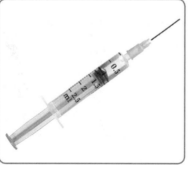

3 ....
....

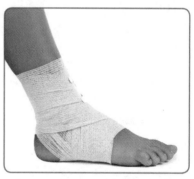

4 ....
....

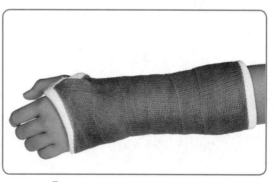

5 ....
....

Vocabulary

Inventions

Unit vocabulary

1 Translate the words.

Machine verbs

attach ....
build ....
communicate ....
invent ....
plug in ....
press ....
produce ....
turn on/off ....

Machine nouns

battery ....
button ....
cable ....
jack ....
keyboard ....
outlet ....
power cord ....
remote control ....
tube ....
wheel ....

2 Translate the words.

Word building

build – builder – building
....

design – designer – design
....

invent – inventor – invention
....

paint – painter – painting
....

produce – producer – product
....

write – writer – writing
....

Vocabulary extension

3 Match the photos to these words. Use your dictionary if necessary. Write the words in English and in your language.

> composer   enter key   function key   sale   ~~unplug~~

1 .... *unplug* ....
....

2 ....
....

3 ....
....

4 ....
....

5 ....
....

Speaking and Listening

Describing a place

• Speaking

1 **Complete the text with these phrases.**
42 **Then listen and check.**

big fireplace	big windows	closet
comfortable	~~pretty new~~	very narrow
wooden ceilings		

Welcome to the old castle! This is the main entrance, between these two towers. The towers look a little strange, because many parts of them are ¹*pretty new*. The windows are ²................... , and they don't have any glass. If we go inside, we can see the main buildings on the left. The building with the really ³........................ is the Great Hall. It has six fireplaces, and tables and chairs for a hundred people! The building opposite the Hall is for the royal apartments. The apartments have high ⁴........................ , walls covered in special cloths called tapestries, and rugs on the floor. Each room has a ⁵........................ to keep people warm and, of course, a very ⁶........................ bed. There isn't very much furniture, usually just a dresser and a ⁷........................ .

2 **Complete the conversation with these phrases.**
43 **Then listen and check.**

| kind of small | ~~like~~ | original |
| uncomfortable | very expensive | what |

A What's that new café ¹*like*?

B You mean the Skyspace?

A Yes, that's it. I've heard it has some really ²........................ decoration.

B That's what Cindy says, too. She told me it has a blue ceiling with stars painted on it.

A Wow! So ³........................ are the tables and chairs like?

B The tables are painted yellow like the sun, but they're ⁴........................ .

A OK!

B And the chairs look like stars, but they're really ⁵........................ .

A Huh. What about the prices?

B Cindy says things are ⁶........................ . A coffee costs three bucks, for example.

A Yikes! Forget it! We'll go to the café at the station.

• Listening

3 **Listen and complete the sentences.**
44 1 Laura is staying in a hotel on the
....

2 She's going on vacation with her
....

3 Frank and Laura can see the hotel in some
....

4 The rooms have a .... with a table and chairs.

5 Frank isn't interested in playing .... at this kind of hotel.

6 Frank doesn't like playing .... at school.

7 There's a club for .... at the hotel.

4 **Listen again. Who says these phrases? Write F**
44 **for Frank or L for Laura.**

1 What's it like?   ....

2 look at the view!   ....

3 four tennis courts   ....

4 Not at school!   ....

5 What about nightlife?   ....

6 That sounds like fun!   ....

Speaking and Listening

Permission

• Speaking

1 **Match the questions (1–6) to the answers (a–f).**
45 **Then listen and check.**

1 Can I stay overnight at Maria's house?   c
2 Do you mind if we park here?
3 Is it OK if I wear jeans?
4 Can we invite some friends for the weekend?
5 Do you mind if I come home late?
6 Is it OK if we make pizza?

a No, I'm sorry, it isn't. You need something
   more formal.
b No, I don't mind. But not later than
   eleven o'clock.
c Yes, you can. But call me in the morning.
d Go ahead! I'll have one with four cheeses.
e No, you can't. We're going away
   this weekend.
f Yes, I do! This is the entrance to a garage!

2 **Complete the conversation with these phrases.**
46 **Then listen and check.**

Can we do	Do you mind	Go ahead
I'm sorry	take photos	Yes, of course

A Bankside Vacation Rentals! Can I help you?
B I'd like to ask a few questions, please.
A ¹ *Go ahead*!
B Is it OK if we ²........................ of
   the apartment?
A ³........................ ! Most people take
   vacation pictures.
B That's fine! And what about uploading them
   on the Internet? ⁴........................ that?
A Sure. That's not a problem.
B Great! And what about pets? ⁵........................
   if we bring a pet?
A What kind of pet? ⁶........................ , we can't
   accept large animals.
B It's just a cat.
A Yes, that's OK, but only on the balcony.
B Thank you!

• Listening

3 **Listen and choose the correct options.**
47 1 The mother is (happy) / *unhappy* for the boy
      to see the photos.
   2 The photos are in *a box* / *an album*.
   3 The grandma died in *1970* / *1980*.
   4 The grandparents were born *before* /
      after the war.
   5 The *grandpa* / *grandma* was an electrician.

4 **Listen again. Put the phrases in the order**
47 **you hear them.**

a in those days   ....
b might get lost   ....
c When did they live? ....
d just before   ....
e take a look at   .1.

Speaking and Listening

Asking for help

• Speaking

(1) **Put the sentences in the correct order.**
48 **Then listen and check.**

- a Three. What do you think of this one? ....
- b Well, can you hold these while I try the other ones? ....
- c Yeah, I think so, too. ....
- d Lisa! Could you give me a hand with these shirts? *1.*
- e It looks too big for you, actually. ....
- f Sure. What do you want me to do? ....
- g OK! How many do you have? ....

(2) **Complete the conversation with these words.**
49 **Then listen and check.**

can't	cost	~~give~~	lending
looking	No	price	

A Carlos! Could you ¹*give* me a hand at the market? I don't speak much Spanish!

B ² .... problem! What are you ³ .... for?

A Some T-shirts, I think.

B OK. Do you see any that you like?

A Those look all right. Could you ask how much they ⁴ .... ?

B Sure … The vendor says they're $10 each.

A That's a good ⁵ .... ! I'll take five of them, but in different colors.

B That's easy. There you go!

A Oh no! I only have $30! I forgot to go to the bank! Would you mind ⁶ .... me $20 to pay for the T-shirts?

B Sorry, I ⁷ .... ! I didn't bring my wallet. But there's an ATM just around the corner. We can go there.

A OK, let's do that!

• Listening

(3) **Listen and choose the correct options.**
50
1 The girl needs help with her *housework* / *homework*

2 The group *can* / *can't* afford hotels.

3 The problem with camping is the *location* / *weather*.

4 The best alternative is *camping* / *a youth hostel*.

5 The girl *has* / *doesn't have* her cell phone with her.

(4) **Listen again. Put the phrases in the order**
50 **you hear them.**

- a Could you think of a better way? ....
- b she forgot to bring it back ....
- c Everyone can afford that! ....
- d Check how much you have to pay ....
- e Are you busy? *1.*
- f I'll check that out now. ....

Speaking and Listening 4

Doubt and disbelief

• Speaking

1 **Put the sentences in the correct order.**
51 **Then listen and check.**

a What are you reading?   .1.
b And what does it say?   ....
c Let me check. Oops! I've sent 45!   ....
d It says that high school students send
  about 30 text messages a day.   ....
e A magazine report about young people
  and cell phones.   ....
f I don't believe it! I've only sent about
  20 messages today. And you?   ....

2 **Complete the conversation with these phrases.**
52 **Then listen and check.**

a strange figure	~~believe~~	impossible
just a statue	kidding	No! Really
That's strange		

A Have you read this report about a ghost
in the local museum?
B I don't ¹ *believe* it!
A It's been in the national news as well.
B ² .... ? What's the story?
A It says people have seen ³ ....
in the museum. And that there have been
reports like this for many years.
B Well, I've never heard of them! Does the
figure move, or is it ⁴ .... ?
A They say it moves around different parts of
the museum.
B That's ⁵ .... ! You would see it
on the video cameras!
A But there aren't any video cameras!
B ⁶ .... ! Most museums have them.
Listen! Why don't we spend the night there
with a camera?
A You're ⁷ .... ! They wouldn't let us
do that!

• Listening

3 **Listen and match the key words (1–5)**
53 **to the words (a–e).**

1 vampire   a dates
2 Germany   b Happy Birthday
3 lose   c semifinals
4 dog   d trailer
5 concert   e match

4 **Listen again. Put the phrases in the order**
53 **you hear them.**

a What about France?   ....
b You're kidding!   ....
c Anything else?   ....
d That's news to me!   ....
e I expected that!   1.
f I don't believe it!   ....

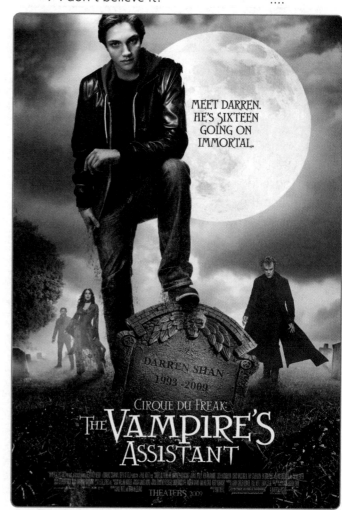

Speaking and Listening

Asking for information

• Speaking

1 **Put the words in order. Then listen and check.**
54

A [1] me / Excuse / us / Can / help / you / ! / ?
Excuse me! Can you help us?
B Sure!
A [2] to / T-shirts / good / a / Where's / buy / place / ?
....
B There's a souvenir shop near the station.
A [3] can / there / get / we / And / how / ?
....
B It's a five-minute walk.
A [4] there / money / there / get / a / bank / to / Is / ?
....
B There's one inside the station.
A [5] take / zoo / How / get / does / to / long / it / the / to / ?
....
B About fifteen minutes by bus.

2 **Complete the conversation with these phrases.**
55 **Then listen and check.**

About twenty minutes	~~for a long time~~
here you go	kind of far
not too expensive	over there
The best way	

A Excuse me! Can you help us? We're looking for the zoo.
B The zoo? I haven't been there [1] *for a long time*! Do you have a map?
A Yes, [2] ....
B OK, let's see. This is where we are now, and that's the zoo [3] ....
A Is it far?
B It's [4] .... , yes.
A How can we get there?
B [5] .... is probably by bus. There's a bus every quarter of an hour.
A How long does it take?
B [6] ....
A Is there a good place to eat at the zoo?

B Yes, there's a cafeteria, and it's [7] ....
A Thank you very much. That's really helpful!

• Listening

3 **You will hear four conversations. Match the**
56 **conversations (1–4) to the topics (a–d).**

a the beach   ....
b an art gallery   *1*
c sunglasses   ....
d a theme park   ....

4 **Listen again. Are the statements true (T)**
56 **or false (F)?**

Conversation 1
1 Speaker 2 can't answer the question.   *T*

Conversation 2
2 Speaker 1 prefers the taxi.   ....

Conversation 3
3 Speaker 2 recommends the pharmacy.   ....

Conversation 4
4 There's a bus every half hour.   ....

Speaking and Listening

Giving advice

• Speaking

1 **Put the conversation in the correct order.**
57 **Then listen and check.**

a What's the matter? Is there anything
  I can do? .1..

b Well, why don't you look in the car? ....

c Did you come home on the bus yesterday? ....

d Maybe you should check your room. ....

e Good idea! Why didn't I think of that?
  Thanks! ....

f No, I didn't. My mom drove me home. ....

g I lost Jill's present. She'll be really upset! ....

h I've looked there three times! ....

2 **Complete the conversation with these phrases.**
58 **Then listen and check.**

| don't have to | I won't see | Why don't you |
| you should let | ~~you should worry~~ | |

A You don't look very happy! What's the
  matter?

B I've found out that Cheryl's having a party,
  and she hasn't invited me!

A I don't think ¹*you should worry* about that.
  Other people have parties, too.

B Yes, but Olivia's going, and if I can't go,
  ² .... her!

A OK, I understand. But you ³ ....
  go to a party to see her.

B That's true, but our class schedules at school
  are very different.

A ⁴ .... call Cheryl and ask her
  for an invitation?

B I'd be too embarrassed!

A All right, maybe ⁵ .... me ask
  her then.

B Will you?

A Sure. Anything for a friend!

B Thanks!

• Listening

3 **Listen to the conversation. Choose**
59 **the correct options.**

1 The *boy /* *girl* is fed up.

2 The girl has to take care of *her parents' /*
  her brother's dog.

3 She has to *feed and wash / feed and walk*
  the dog.

4 The boy offers the girl *one solution /*
  two solutions to the problem.

5 The boy has a *cat / dog.*

4 **Listen again. Who says these phrases? Write B**
59 **for the boy or G for the girl.**

1 What's new with you? .B.

2 What's the matter? ....

3 It's not fair! ....

4 just tell me ....

5 That's great ....

Persuading

• Speaking

(1) **Put the words in the correct order. Then listen**
60 **and check.**

A Let's go and take up a collection. Come on.
   ¹ fun / It'll / be / !
   It'll be fun!

B I'm not so sure about that.

A I don't really want to design banners for you.

B ² better / It's / doing / nothing / than / !

....

A But we don't know how to make signs.

B ³ can / quickly / sure / we / I'm / learn

....

A What about a petition?

B ⁴ know / idea / I / if / good / that's / a / don't

....

A I'm sure you'll do a great job.

B ⁵ it / do / OK, / I'll / !

....

(2) **Complete the conversation with these phrases.**
61 **Then listen and check.**

I don't know	~~If I paint the slogans~~
I'm not sure about	it'll be fun
it's better than	

A We need to make some signs for next
   weekend!

B Who's "we," Dad?

A You and me, of course.

B But it's your sit-in, Dad. You're organizing it.

A And if I lose my job, you won't get any
   allowance! ¹ *If I paint the slogans*, will you cut
   the wood?

B ² .... , Dad.

A Come on, ³ .... to work together!

B But you know I'm allergic to sawdust!

A I know that you *say* you're allergic! OK,
   I'll cut the wood, but you'll have to paint
   the slogans!

B ⁴ .... that.

A Well, ⁵ .... walking home after
   your party tonight, isn't it?

B All right, you win. I'll do it!

• Listening

(3) **Listen to the conversation and complete the**
62 **summary. Use one word in each space.**

The girl wants her mother to go to
a ¹ *fundraising* event with her. She wants to help
a ² .... , but her mother doesn't really
³ .... to go. The mother wants
the girl to help her ⁴ .... the sheets,
but the girl ⁵ .... like that idea.
In the end, the mother ⁶ .... the
girl to help, and they both go out together.

(4) **Listen again. Who says these phrases?**
62 **Write M for mother or D for daughter.**

1 a little busy   *M*
2 for a charity   ....
3 I'll tell you what.   ....
4 not good at that   ....
5 you'll learn quickly   ....

Speaking and Listening

Talking about health

• Speaking

1 **Choose the correct options. Then listen and check.**

63

1 **A** What's wrong with you?
   B My forehead is *burning hot* / *exhausted*!
   I think I have a fever.

2 **A** What's the matter with you?
   B I feel *exhausted* / *terrifying*!

3 **A** You don't look well!
   B I'm not! I just got a *burn* / *cold* on my leg!

4 **A** You look awful!
   B And I *matter* / *feel* awful! I have a headache and a bad cough.

5 **A** How do you feel?
   B I got up with a terrible backache, but I'm feeling *not too well* / *a little better* now.

2 **Complete the conversation with these phrases. Then listen and check.**

64

a little better	~~Are you all right~~
drink some of this	How does it feel
sore throat	

A Hey! ¹ *Are you all right*?
B No, I'm not. I have a really ² ....
A Where did you get that?
B I'm not sure. Maybe it was the concert last night.
A Hold on a minute. Here, ³ .... That should help you.
B What is it?
A It's something my grandma makes for colds and sore throats. ⁴ .... ?
B It tastes really bitter!
A Yes, but what about your throat?
B Oh, that's ⁵ .... already, thanks.

• Listening

3 **Listen and choose the correct options.**

65

1 Andy hurt himself *playing soccer* / *walking*.
2 He got back home by *ambulance* / *car*.
3 *Andy went to the doctor.* / *The doctor visited Andy at home.*
4 Andy has to rest for ten *days* / *weeks*.
5 Trish suggests *going to the movies* / *watching a movie at home.*

4 **Listen again. Put these phrases in the order you hear them.**

65

a That was lucky! ....
b How did you get back? ....
c Why not? ....
d Not too well *1.*
e Poor thing! ....

Speaking and Listening

Problems with machines

● Speaking

1 Choose the correct options. Then listen and check.

66

1 This digital recorder *isn't* / *doesn't* work.

2 I *can't* / *not* listen to the recordings I made.

3 There might be *nothing* / *something* wrong with the battery.

4 Have you *check* / *checked* it?

5 Have you tried *press* / *pressing* the "play" button?

6 You're pressing the *right* / *wrong* button!

2 Complete the conversation with these phrases.

67 Then listen and check.

~~Did you press~~	Have you checked
I tried that	Let me take a look
something wrong	that doesn't work

A What's the matter?

B I can't change the channels on the TV.

A ¹ *Did you press* the right button on the remote control?

B Yes, ² .... , but nothing happens, and it was OK yesterday.

A Have you checked the volume control?

B Yes, and ³ .... either.

A Well, there must be ⁴ .... with the remote control then. ⁵ .... the batteries?

B Yes! I took them out and put them back in again.

A ⁶ .... Hmm, one of the batteries isn't making contact. Let's press it in better. There you go. Try it again.

B Great! It works! Thanks a lot!

● Listening

3 Listen and choose the correct answers.

68

1 The problem with the coffee maker was due to …

a no electricity.

b no coffee.

c no water.

2 The cause of the problem was …

a a visitor.

b a phone call.

c a TV show.

3 The problem lasted between …

a five and ten minutes.

b ten and fifteen minutes.

c ten and twenty minutes.

4 Listen again. Put these phrases in the order

68 you hear them.

a you're lucky ....

b the coffee pot over there ....

c How did that happen? ....

d the red light on ..1..

e That one! ....

Pronunciation

Consonants

Symbol	Example	Your examples
/p/	park	
/b/	big	
/t/	toy	
/d/	dog	
/k/	car	
/g/	good	
/tʃ/	chair	
/dʒ/	jeans	
/f/	farm	
/v/	visit	
/θ/	three	
/ð/	they	
/s/	swim	
/z/	zoo	
/ʃ/	shop	
/ʒ/	television	
/h/	hot	
/m/	map	
/n/	notes	
/ŋ/	sing	
/l/	laptop	
/r/	room	
/y/	yellow	
/w/	watch	

Vowels

Symbol	Example	Your examples
/ɪ/	rich	
/ɛ/	egg	
/æ/	rat	
/ɑ/	job	
/ʌ/	fun	
/ʊ/	put	
/i/	eat	
/eɪ/	gray	
/aɪ/	my	
/ɔɪ/	boy	
/u/	boot	
/oʊ/	note	
/aʊ/	now	
/ɪr/	hear	
/ɛr/	hair	
/ɑr/	star	
/ɔ/	dog	
/ʊr/	tour	
/ɔr/	door	
/ə/	among	
/ɚ/	shirt	

Pronunciation practice

Unit 1 • /v/, /w/ and /b/

1 Listen and repeat.

69
1 We will drive these five vans down Bay Avenue.
2 Will you wait for me while I'm away?
3 Meet Bill at the library, and bring your bicycle, too!
4 Put the books in the bookcase and the bike on the balcony.
5 Put the heavy vases on the living room floor.
6 We always travel abroad for our winter break.

2 Put words from Exercise 1 in the correct column.
69 **Then listen again and check.**

/v/	/w/	/b/
drive	we	Bay
....	....	....
....	....	....
....	....	....
....	....	....

Unit 2 • Sentence stress

1 Listen and repeat the stressed words.

70
1 What – do
2 What – do – work
3 What – doing
4 What – doing – morning
5 doing – homework – room
6 wasn't – games – laptop

2 Listen again and write the sentences.

70
1 ....
2 ....
3 ....
4 ....
5 ....
6 ....

3 Listen again and repeat the complete sentences.
70

Unit 3 • /ɔ/ and /oʊ/

1 Listen and repeat.

71
1 We bought all the donuts in the store!
2 I don't know!
3 This coat is too short for me.
4 No cell phones in here!
5 He lost his dog in the forest.
6 Don't go home now!

2 Put words from Exercise 1 in the correct column.
71 **Then listen again and check.**

/ɔ/	/oʊ/
bought	donuts
....	....
....	....
....	....
....	....
....	....

Unit 4 • /æ/ and /ɑ/

1 Listen and repeat.

72
1 You can't charge your laptop batteries in the café!
2 Carry the backpacks please, Sam!
3 They ran into a traffic jam on the way to the park.
4 That's the first album she sang with the band.

2 Put words from Exercise 1 in the correct column.
72 **Then listen again and check.**

/æ/	/ɑ/
can't	charge
....	....
....	....
....	....
....	....
....	....
....	....

Unit 5 • /aɪ/ vs /ɪ/

1 **Listen and repeat.**

73
1 There'll be bright sunshine in the five islands.
2 The interactive visit begins at six.
3 When I go by bike, I usually arrive on time.
4 It's a pretty little village in Italy.

2 **Put words from Exercise 1 in the correct column.**
73 **Then listen again and check.**

/aɪ/	/ɪ/
bright	in
....	....
....	....
....	....
....	....

Unit 6 • /ʌ/ and /yu/

1 **Listen and repeat.**

74
1 My uncle makes beautiful sculptures.
2 There is a ton of music online.
3 There's a long line outside the new museum.
4 I usually get up early and go running
on Sundays.

2 **Put words from Exercise 1 in the correct column.**
74 **Then listen again and check.**

/ʌ/	/yu/
uncle	beautiful
....	....
....	....
....	....

Unit 7 • Going to

1 **Listen to the recording. Underline the sentences**
75 **where you hear _gonna_ instead of _going to_.**

A What are you going to do today?
B I'm going to a demonstration.
A What are you going to do there?
B I'm going to hold a sign and chant slogans.
A Are you going to a restaurant there?

B I'm not going to make plans right now.
A What time are you going to come back?
B I dunno. I'm just going to take it easy.

2 **Listen again and repeat. First A, then B.**
75

Unit 8 • gh

1 **Listen and repeat the sentences.**

76
1 He caught eight fish, and that was enough.
2 They didn't laugh because they were frightened.
3 My daughter is sick and coughs a lot.
4 They taught me that "rough" is the opposite
of "smooth."

2 **Put words from Exercise 1 with _gh_ in the correct**
76 **column. Then listen again and check.**

/f/	silent
enough	caught
....	....
....	....
....	....

Unit 9 • /ɪ/ and /i/

1 **Listen and repeat the sentences.**

77
1 Please keep your feet off the table!
2 Don't swim in the river—it's really deep!
3 I'd like three kilos of green peas.
4 If it isn't in there, then I can't think where it is!

2 **Put words from Exercise 1 with the corresponding**
77 **sounds in the correct column. Then listen again**
and check.

/ɪ/	/i/
swim	Please
....	....
....	....
....	....
....	....
....	....
....	....

Irregular Verb List

Verb	Past Simple	Past Participle
be	was/were	been
become	became	become
begin	began	begun
break	broke	broken
bring	brought	brought
build	built	built
buy	bought	bought
can	could	been able
catch	caught	caught
choose	chose	chosen
come	came	come
cost	cost	cost
cut	cut	cut
do	did	done
draw	drew	drawn
drink	drank	drunk
drive	drove	driven
eat	ate	eaten
fall	fell	fallen
feed	fed	fed
feel	felt	felt
fight	fought	fought
find	found	found
fly	flew	flown
forget	forgot	forgotten
get	got	gotten
give	gave	given
go	went	gone/been
have	had	had
hear	heard	heard
hold	held	held
keep	kept	kept
know	knew	known
leave	left	left
lend	lent	lent

Verb	Past Simple	Past Participle
light	lit	lit
lose	lost	lost
make	made	made
mean	meant	meant
meet	met	met
pay	paid	paid
put	put	put
read /riːd/	read /rɛd/	read /rɛd/
ride	rode	ridden
ring	rang	rung
run	ran	run
say	said	said
see	saw	seen
sell	sold	sold
send	sent	sent
shine	shone	shone
show	showed	shown
sing	sang	sung
sit	sat	sat
sleep	slept	slept
speak	spoke	spoken
spend	spent	spent
stand	stood	stood
steal	stole	stolen
swim	swam	swum
take	took	taken
teach	taught	taught
tell	told	told
think	thought	thought
throw	threw	thrown
understand	understood	understood
wake	woke	woken
wear	wore	worn
win	won	won
write	wrote	written

My Assessment Profile Starter Unit

1 **What can I do? Mark (✓) the options in the table.**

⏪ = I need to study this again.　⏸ = I'm not sure about this.　▶ = I'm happy with this.　⏩ = I do this very well.

		⏪	⏸	▶	⏩
Vocabulary (Student's Book pages 4–7)	• I can use common verbs correctly. • I can use prepositions correctly. • I can talk about everyday objects. • I can talk about school subjects. • I can talk about numbers and dates. • I can use opinion adjectives correctly.				
Reading (SB page 9)	• I can understand profiles on a school intranet page.				
Grammar (SB pages 4–7)	• I can use all forms of *to be* in the Present simple. • I can use all forms of *have* in the Present simple. • I can use the possessive *'s* correctly. • I can tell the difference between possessive *'s* and the contraction *'s*. • I can use subject and object pronouns correctly. • I can use possessive adjectives correctly. • I can use indefinite pronouns correctly. • I can use the Present simple correctly. • I can use adverbs of frequency correctly. • I can use *was/were* correctly.				
Speaking (SB page 8)	• I can ask for and give personal information.				
Listening (SB page 8)	• I can understand conversations about personal information.				
Writing (SB page 9)	• I can write a personal profile.				

2 **What new words and expressions can I remember?**

words ....

expressions ....

3 **How can I practice other new words and expressions?**

record them on my MP3 player ☐　　　write them in a notebook ☐

practice them with a friend ☐　　　translate them into my language ☐

4 **What English have I learned outside class?**

	words	expressions
on the radio		
in songs		
in movies		
on the Internet		
on TV		
with friends		

My Assessment Profile Unit

1 **What can I do? Mark (✓) the options in the table.**

◄◄ = I need to study this again.　❚❚ = I'm not sure about this.　▶ = I'm happy with this.　▶▶ = I do this very well.

		◄◄	❚❚	▶	▶▶
Vocabulary (Student's Book pages 10 and 13)	• I can talk about rooms and parts of the house. • I can talk about furniture and household objects.				
Pronunciation (SB page 13)	• I can understand and say correctly the sounds /v/, /w/ and /b/.				
Reading (SB pages 11 and 16)	• I can understand articles about houses and rooms.				
Grammar (SB pages 12 and 15)	• I can use the Present simple and Present continuous correctly. • I can use verbs with the -ing form correctly.				
Speaking (SB pages 14 and 15)	• I can describe a place.				
Listening (SB page 16)	• I can understand a person describing her room.				
Writing (SB page 17)	• I can link similar and contrasting ideas. • I can write a description of a room.				

2 **What new words and expressions can I remember?**

words ....

expressions ....

3 **How can I practice other new words and expressions?**

record them on my MP3 player ☐　　　write them in a notebook ☐

practice them with a friend ☐　　　translate them into my language ☐

4 **What English have I learned outside class?**

	words	expressions
on the radio		
in songs		
in movies		
on the Internet		
on TV		
with friends		

My Assessment Profile   Unit

1 What can I do? Mark (✓) the options in the table.

◄◄ = I need to study this again.　 ❚❚ = I'm not sure about this.　 ► = I'm happy with this.　 ►► = I do this very well.

		◄◄	❚❚	►	►►
Vocabulary (Student's Book pages 20 and 23)	• I can use adjectives to describe pictures. • I can use adjectives with prepositions.				
Pronunciation (SB page 23)	• I can hear stressed words in sentences and say sentences with the correct stress.				
Reading (SB pages 21 and 26)	• I can understand descriptions of pictures and stories behind the pictures.				
Grammar (SB pages 22, 23 and 25)	• I can use the Past simple and Past continuous correctly.				
Speaking (SB pages 24 and 25)	• I can ask for and give permission.				
Listening (SB page 26)	• I can understand people talking about a famous photo.				
Writing (SB page 27)	• I can locate people and things in a picture. • I can write a description of a picture.				

2 What new words and expressions can I remember?

words ....

expressions ....

3 How can I practice other new words and expressions?

record them on my MP3 player ☐　　write them in a notebook ☐

practice them with a friend ☐　　translate them into my language ☐

4 What English have I learned outside class?

	words	expressions
on the radio		
in songs		
in movies		
on the Internet		
on TV		
with friends		

My Assessment Profile Unit

1 What can I do? Mark (✓) the options in the table.

⏪ = I need to study this again.   ⏸ = I'm not sure about this.   ▶ = I'm happy with this.   ⏩ = I do this very well.

		⏪	⏸	▶	⏩
Vocabulary (Student's Book pages 30 and 33)	• I can talk about shopping. • I can use shopping nouns and money verbs.				
Pronunciation (SB page 33)	• I can understand and say correctly the sounds /ɔ/ and /oʊ/.				
Reading (SB pages 31 and 36)	• I can understand articles about shopping.				
Grammar (SB pages 32 and 35)	• I can use comparatives and superlatives correctly. • I can use *too* and *enough* correctly. • I can use *much, many* and *a lot of* correctly.				
Speaking (SB pages 34 and 35)	• I can ask for help and respond.				
Listening (SB page 36)	• I can understand a radio news report.				
Writing (SB page 37)	• I can express my opinion in writing. • I can write a customer review.				

2 What new words and expressions can I remember?

words ....

expressions ....

3 How can I practice other new words and expressions?

record them on my MP3 player ☐   write them in a notebook ☐

practice them with a friend ☐   translate them into my language ☐

4 What English have I learned outside class?

	words	expressions
on the radio		
in songs		
in movies		
on the Internet		
on TV		
with friends		

My Assessment Profile   Unit

1 **What can I do? Mark (✓) the options in the table.**

 = I need to study this again.   ❚❚ = I'm not sure about this.   ▶ = I'm happy with this.   ▶▶ = I do this very well.

		◀◀	❚❚	▶	▶▶
Vocabulary (Student's Book pages 44 and 47)	• I can talk about news and the media. • I can use adverbs of manner.				
Pronunciation (SB page 47)	• I can understand and say correctly the sounds /æ/ and /ɑ/.				
Reading (SB pages 45 and 50)	• I can understand newspaper and magazine reports.				
Grammar (SB pages 46 and 49)	• I can use the Present perfect correctly. • I know when to use the Present perfect and when to use the Past simple.				
Speaking (SB pages 48 and 49)	• I can express doubt and disbelief.				
Listening (SB page 50)	• I can understand different people talking about the news.				
Writing (SB page 51)	• I can check spelling, punctuation and grammar. • I can write a profile.				

2 **What new words and expressions can I remember?**

words ....

expressions ....

3 **How can I practice other new words and expressions?**

record them on my MP3 player ☐   write them in a notebook ☐

practice them with a friend ☐   translate them into my language ☐

4 **What English have I learned outside class?**

	words	expressions
on the radio		
in songs		
in movies		
on the Internet		
on TV		
with friends		

My Assessment Profile   Unit

1 **What can I do? Mark (✓) the options in the table.**

⏪ = I need to study this again.   ⏸ = I'm not sure about this.   ▶ = I'm happy with this.   ⏩ = I do this very well.

		⏪	⏸	▶	⏩
Vocabulary (Student's Book pages 54 and 57)	• I can talk about vacations. • I know different meanings of the verb *get*.				
Pronunciation (SB page 56)	• I can understand and say correctly the sounds /aɪ/ and /ɪ/.				
Reading (SB pages 55 and 60)	• I can understand stories about travel experiences and tourist attractions.				
Grammar (SB pages 56 and 59)	• I can use the Present perfect with *for* and *since* correctly. • I can use the Past simple with *just*. • I can ask questions with *How long?*				
Speaking (SB pages 58 and 59)	• I can ask for information.				
Listening (SB page 60)	• I can understand a radio show about unusual hotels.				
Writing (SB page 61)	• I can use adjectives and new vocabulary in my writing. • I can write a travel guide.				

2 **What new words and expressions can I remember?**

words ....

expressions ....

3 **How can I practice other new words and expressions?**

record them on my MP3 player ☐   write them in a notebook ☐

practice them with a friend ☐   translate them into my language ☐

4 **What English have I learned outside class?**

	words	expressions
on the radio		
in songs		
in movies		
on the Internet		
on TV		
with friends		

My Assessment Profile Unit

1 **What can I do? Mark (✓) the options in the table.**

⏪ = I need to study this again. ⏸ = I'm not sure about this. ▶ = I'm happy with this. ⏩ = I do this very well.

		⏪	⏸	▶	⏩
Vocabulary (Student's Book pages 64 and 67)	• I can talk about household chores. • I can use adjectives to describe feelings.				
Pronunciation (SB page 67)	• I can understand and say correctly the sounds /ʌ/ and /yu/.				
Reading (SB pages 65 and 70)	• I can understand articles about household chores.				
Grammar (SB pages 66, 67 and 69)	• I can use verbs to express obligation, no obligation and prohibition correctly. • I can make predictions with *will*, *won't* and *might*.				
Speaking (SB pages 68 and 69)	• I can give advice.				
Listening (SB page 70)	• I can understand conversations between teenagers of the future.				
Writing (SB page 71)	• I can explain reasons and results. • I can write a letter of advice.				

2 **What new words and expressions can I remember?**

words ....

expressions ....

3 **How can I practice other new words and expressions?**

record them on my MP3 player ☐   write them in a notebook ☐

practice them with a friend ☐   translate them into my language ☐

4 **What English have I learned outside class?**

	words	expressions
on the radio		
in songs		
in movies		
on the Internet		
on TV		
with friends		

My Assessment Profile   Unit

1 **What can I do? Mark (✓) the options in the table.**

⏪ = I need to study this again.   ⏸ = I'm not sure about this.   ▶ = I'm happy with this.   ⏩ = I do this very well.

		⏪	⏸	▶	⏩
Vocabulary (Student's Book pages 78 and 81)	• I can talk about protest and support. • I can use verbs with prepositions.				
Pronunciation (SB page 80)	• I can hear the difference between *gonna* and *going to*.				
Reading (SB pages 79 and 84)	• I can understand articles about protest and support issues.				
Grammar (SB pages 80, 81 and 83)	• I can use *be going to* and *will* correctly. • I can use the First conditional.				
Speaking (SB pages 82 and 83)	• I can persuade someone to do something.				
Listening (SB page 84)	• I can understand an interview about a charity.				
Writing (SB page 85)	• I can format a letter or email correctly. • I can write a formal letter.				

2 **What new words and expressions can I remember?**

words ....

expressions ....

3 **How can I practice other new words and expressions?**

record them on my MP3 player ☐   write them in a notebook ☐

practice them with a friend ☐   translate them into my language ☐

4 **What English have I learned outside class?**

	words	expressions
on the radio		
in songs		
in movies		
on the Internet		
on TV		
with friends		

My Assessment Profile   Unit

1 **What can I do? Mark (✓) the options in the table.**

◄◄ = I need to study this again.   ❚❚ = I'm not sure about this.   ▶ = I'm happy with this.   ▶▶ = I do this very well.

		◄◄	❚❚	▶	▶▶
Vocabulary (Student's Book pages 88 and 91)	• I can use extreme adjectives. • I can talk about illness and injury.				
Pronunciation (SB page 91)	• I can hear the difference between *gh* with the sound /f/ and silent *gh*.				
Reading (SB pages 89 and 94)	• I can understand articles about danger and risk.				
Grammar (SB pages 90 and 93)	• I can use the Second conditional correctly. • I can use relative pronouns.				
Speaking (SB pages 92 and 93)	• I can talk about health.				
Listening (SB page 94)	• I can understand a conversation about an adventure game show.				
Writing (SB page 95)	• I can interpret an application form. • I can fill in an application form correctly.				

2 **What new words and expressions can I remember?**

words ....

expressions ....

3 **How can I practice other new words and expressions?**

record them on my MP3 player ☐   write them in a notebook ☐

practice them with a friend ☐   translate them into my language ☐

4 **What English have I learned outside class?**

	words	expressions
on the radio		
in songs		
in movies		
on the Internet		
on TV		
with friends		

My Assessment Profile   Unit (9)

1 What can I do? Mark (✓) the options in the table.

⏪ = I need to study this again.   ⏸ = I'm not sure about this.   ▶ = I'm happy with this.   ⏩ = I do this very well.

		⏪	⏸	▶	⏩
Vocabulary (Student's Book pages 98 and 101)	• I can talk about machines. • I can use machine-related nouns and verbs.				
Pronunciation (SB page 101)	• I can understand and say correctly the sounds /ɪ/ and /i/.				
Reading (SB pages 99 and 104)	• I can understand articles about machines and inventions.				
Grammar (SB pages 100 and 103)	• I can use the Present simple passive and Past simple passive correctly. • I know when to use *by* in passive sentences.				
Speaking (SB page 104)	• I can talk about problems with machines.				
Listening (SB pages 102 and 103)	• I can understand a conversation about the advantages and disadvantages of reading on a smart phone.				
Writing (SB page 105)	• I can organize an opinion essay. • I can write an opinion essay with reasons and examples.				

2 What new words and expressions can I remember?

words ....

expressions ....

3 How can I practice other new words and expressions?

record them on my MP3 player ☐   write them in a notebook ☐

practice them with a friend ☐   translate them into my language ☐

4 What English have I learned outside class?

	words	expressions
on the radio		
in songs		
in movies		
on the Internet		
on TV		
with friends		

Pearson Education Limited
Edinburgh Gate
Harlow
Essex CM20 2JE
England
and Associated Companies throughout the world.

www.pearsonelt.com/moveit

Printed and bound in Poland by Zapolex
First published 2015, Thirteenth impression 2022
Set in 10.5/12.5pt LTC Helvetica Neue Light
ISBN: 978-1-4479-8341-5

Photo Acknowledgements
The publisher would like to thank the following for their kind permission to reproduce their photographs:

(Key: b-bottom; c-centre; l-left; r-right; t-top)

Alamy Images: allesalltag 106b, Archimage 25t, Arco Images GmbH 40, blickwinkel 17b, Mark Boulton 110cr, Cliff Hide News 119, Ashley Cooper 69, Ian Dagnall 82c, Gallo Images 55, Nikolay Mihalchenko 109cr, Mode Images 50, Christine Nichols 17c, NielsVK 77, redsnapper 121, Andre Seale 83, SuperStock 25b, Colin Underhill 106tr, 110tl, vario images GmbH & Co.K 45, Tony Watson 113, way out west photography 108tr, Young-Wolff Photography 35t; **Bridgeman Art Library Ltd:** The Yellow House, 1888 (oil on canvas), Gogh, Vincent van (1853-90) / Van Gogh Museum, Amsterdam, The Netherlands 48; **Corbis:** cultura / Monty Rakusen 105cl, cultura / Nancy Honey 112b, Bob Krist 114; **Fotolia.com:** 126-135, withGod 35b; **FotoLibra:** Nicola Mary Barranger 109cl, Mkimages 104b; **Getty Images:** Cultura / Ghislain & Marie David de Lossy 108cr, Digital Vision / Alistair Berg 109b, Digital Vision / Paul Burns 105cr, Taxi / Javier Pierini 56, Lifesize / John Howard 109tr, Lifesize / Maria Teijeiro 23, Stockbyte / Jae Rew 30, StockImage / Bernard Jaubert 17t, Stone / Art Wolfe 110tr, The Image Bank / Britt Erlanson 105b, The Image Bank / Larry Dale Gordon 120; **Pearson Education Ltd:** Gareth Boden 80; **Press Association Images:** AP / Brynjar Gauti 22, AP / Leanne Italie 66; **Rex Features:** Image Broker 82t, Sipa / Di Crollalanza 41, Ray Tang 106cr; **Science Photo Library Ltd:** Sinclair Stammers 108b; **Shutterstock.com:** alanf 49, Yuri Arcurs 112cr, Bambuh 111cl, Stacy Barnett 111b, Nick Biemans 1, Blend Images 111tl, CandyBox Images 109tl, Hung Chung Chih 110cl, Corepics VOF, CristinaMuraca 9, Dean Drobot 39, Jaimie Duplass 106cl, Edw 118, Francois Etienne du Plessis 107b, Anton Gvozdikov 73, hansenn 74, Kitch Bain 104tr, Kokhanchikov 104tl, Lakeview Images 110b, Lance Bellers 108tl, Petr Malyshev 82b, michaeljung 43, Monkey Business Images 13t, 61, oksana2010 111cr, photobar 107t, Photoseeker 104cl, Rechitan Sorin 104cr, Heidi Schneider 105tr, Lana Smirnova 108cl, Tristan Tan 117, THPStock 106tl, Tupungato 115, Alex Yeung 14, Olena Zaskochenko 13b; **SuperStock:** Scott Stulberg 105tl, Zefa 78; **The Kobal Collection:** Universal Pictures 116; **Veer / Corbis:** Adrian Britton 112tl, Roman Ivaschenko 112cl, JohnKwan 112tr, smithore 111tr

All other images © Pearson Education

Cover image: *Front:* **Shutterstock.com:** Galina Barskaya

Every effort has been made to trace the copyright holders and we apologise in advance for any unintentional omissions. We would be pleased to insert the appropriate acknowledgement in any subsequent edition of this publication.

Illustrated by: Moreno Chiacchiera pages 4, 5, 8, 11, 15, 34; Peskimo pages 10, 24, 39, 50, 60, 65, 107; Paula Franco pages 19, 27, 29, 47, 63, 71, 73.